CW01301769

# Field Marshal Rommel's Trip Home
## June 4, 1944

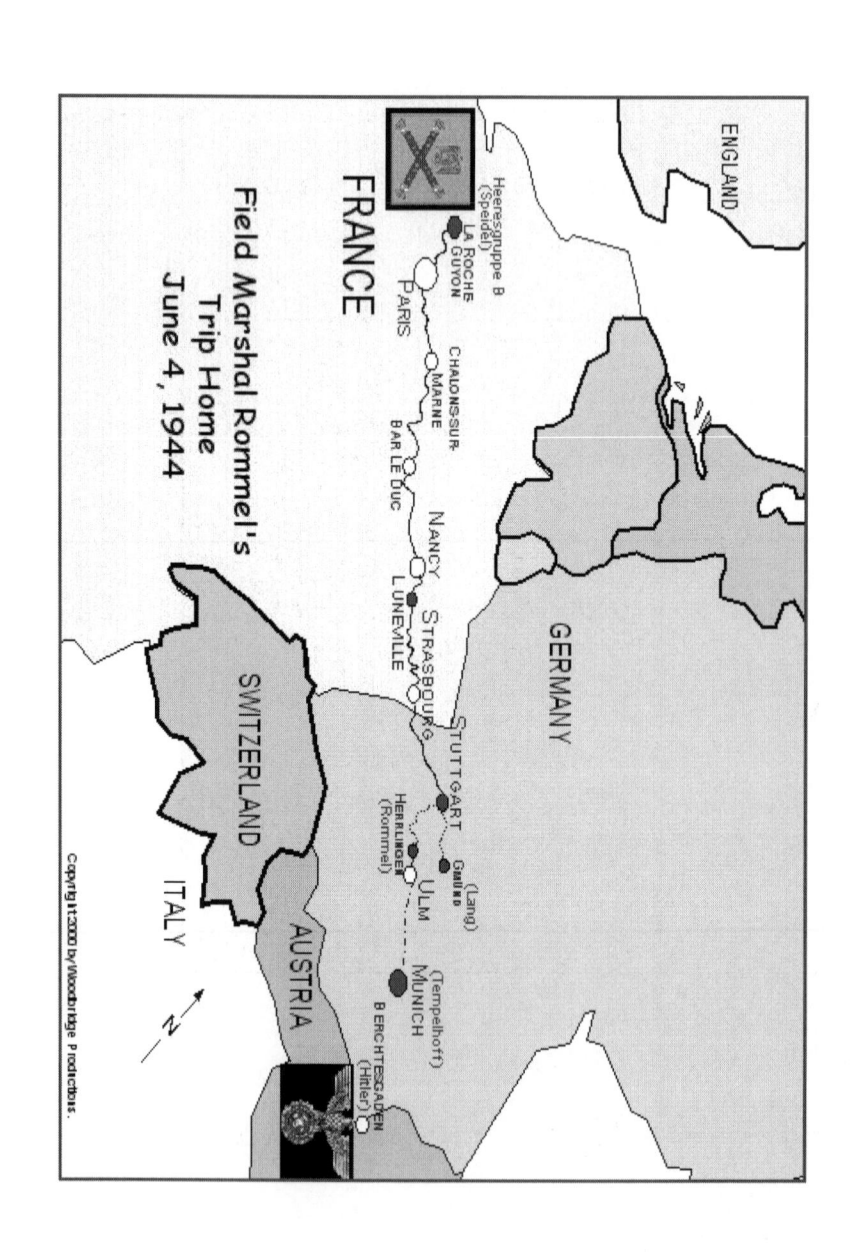

# Rommel's Fateful Trip Home
## June 4th to June 6th, 1944

### By Peter Margaritis

Copyright 2000, 2014, and 2015 by Peter Margaritis

All rights reserved. No portion of this material may be copied, reproduced, transmitted, or reused in any medium or form without expressed written consent by the author.

3rd Edition. Printed in the United States of America.

ISBN-13: 978-1511500418
ISBN-10: 1511500417

Cover photo courtesy of U.S. National Archives, Washington, D.C.

Preface ........................................................................... v
I. June 1st through the 3rd .............................................. 1
II. June 4th—The Trip Home ......................................... 27
III. June 5th .................................................................. 55
IV. June 6th—Morning .................................................. 67
V.- Rommel Heads Back ............................................... 85
VI. D-Day: Evening ...................................................... 95
Epilogue ...................................................................... 111
German Terms Used ................................................... 113
Reference Notes .......................................................... 119
Bibliography ............................................................... 120
Endnotes ..................................................................... 127

## Preface

World War II—the fifth year of the war.

It was early June, 1944. A tired Field Marshal Erwin Rommel—the legendary Desert Fox—commanded the German forces in the northern half of the Reich's Western Theatre. It was his job to defend Western France and the Low Countries from any enemy invasion, and that was a grave responsibility that had weighed heavily on his mind over the last few months.

On June 4th though, a considerable storm was coming in from the Atlantic and rolling onto the continent. Because of this, Rommel was going to take advantage of the bad weather and leave his headquarters on the Seine River to go home for a few days to snatch a bit of well-earned leave. With heavy seas and rain squalls in the English Channel, he was near certain that no invasion was immediately imminent. Although the right combination of tides and moon phase was approaching, a massive successful landing would need in addition, nearly a week of perfect weather. So right now would probably be his last chance to take advantage of the inclement conditions and go home for a short stay before the long-awaited Allied landing came. Besides, it was his wife's fiftieth birthday. Afterwards, he would make a very brief detour down to Lower Bavaria to call on the Führer at his Berghof mountain villa outside of Berchtesgaden. Rommel was going to once more plead with him to release all of the powerful reserve panzer divisions in northern France into his direct control, so that he might better place them strategically for a quicker response.

Unfortunately for the Germans, they could not know that the storm would pass much quicker than they anticipated, and that a brief period of barely fair conditions for a landing would set in. They did not know this because they were no longer getting reliable weather reports from their hidden weather stations in Greenland. This was because over the last couple years, the Allied navies, especially the U.S. Coast Guard, had through a series of deadly hide-and-seek operations, conducted wide-ranging searches over vast areas of Greenland and Iceland. In doing so, they had methodically found or captured several German meteorological units operating there. Those that survived capture had been forced over the months to move and eventually evacuate back to Occupied Europe. Thus, the *Luftwaffe* could no longer accurately predict what type of weather would come in from the Western Atlantic. They could only determine general conditions.

Even so, the Germans might not normally have had to worry that the Allies would take such a chance for this extremely important undertaking. They did not know though, that General Eisenhower, who was surprisingly fully supported by the normally cautious Field Marshal Montgomery, would decide to risk going in the tolerable although tricky weather, instead of opting for the safer delay for possibly better weather down the road. The decision to postpone though was to him even riskier, because there was no guarantee that the next period of required moon and tide conditions would be any better, and the delay could cost them the critical element of surprise. A secret like this could not be kept forever, no matter what the precautions.

Thus as history well knows, on June 6, the mightiest armada in history launched the greatest invasion ever attempted, targeted for the shores of Normandy. For Rommel, what started out as a pleasant trip home would end up as a nightmare of miscalculation and a frantic return to France.

Experts have long-speculated what difference Rommel's presence at the front might have made in those momentous early morning hours of June 6th. In the end, it would all have boiled down to whether he would have been able to get immediate control of the three nearby reserve panzer divisions, direct them to the front, and conduct an immediate, active defense. If he could have, history might very well have turned out differently. Even though the 21st Panzer was less than an hour away from the landing areas, the unit was of inferior quality. However, the nearby 12th SS Panzer and *Panzer Lehr* were massive divisions, strong forces that could move swiftly and hit hard.

The effect of those powerful armored units rolling down onto the incoming Allied soldiers struggling to get off the beaches would have been considerable, especially if the panzers had attacked in a coordinated set of strikes. A massive Allied naval presence notwithstanding, a few dozen buttoned-down Panthers and Mk IV's advancing down upon the hapless Americans laboring to get ashore at Omaha, or onto the plucky Canadians at Juno, could easily have turned the scales.

Add to that the considerable effectiveness of Rommel's experienced on-the-spot direction of the battle as he no doubt would have done, and the invasion might have turned into a disaster. Still, to do so, he would have had to act quickly and decisively, and most importantly, he would have had to convince Hitler to release the panzers to his control.

But of course, that is all just theory, just a whole series of fascinating 'what-ifs.' This is the story of what REALLY happened. A trip that turned out to be a calculated mistake, one that put the famed German commanding general in the wrong place at the wrong time.

All of the facts in this account are directly based upon material thoroughly researched by many historians, and the majority of it comes from first-hand interviews taken of the people involved. I have given this story, as author Joseph E. Persico once wrote, a "strong narrative account" to impart to the reader a better flavor for what actually happened; but all events given are either documented, or very strongly based upon the evidence.

*Peter Margaritis*

# I. June 1st through the 3rd

"...If only the enemy would wait just a few weeks more..."

## Thursday, June 1st

On this early Thursday morning, *Generalfeldmarschall* Erwin Rommel, *Befehlshaber, Heeresgruppe B*,[a] was in his situation room at his château headquarters of La Roche-Guyon, located on the northern bank of the Seine River, some 75 kilometers northwest of Paris. The historic castle had been his headquarters since March, and he and his staff were by now quite comfortable living and working there.

He was studying the latest disposition of his units on the main situation map. Both he and his superior officer, crusty old *Generalfeldmarschall* Gerd von Rundstedt, *OB West*,[b] could be thankful (not to mention quite relieved) that their mobile forces had for the most part been built back up again. Most of their missing panzer divisions had been at various times been moved East in desperate attempts to stave off disaster on the Russian Front. Now they had finally been returned to France to nurse their wounds, rebuild their units, and prepare for the upcoming Allied invasion in the West.

---

[a] Commander, Army Group B. This army group, positioned along the northern part of Western Europe, was responsible for repulsing the expected Allied invasion, and its area of responsibility included the northwestern French coast, from the Belgian border to the Loire Estuary.

[b] *Oberbefehlshaber-West*—Commander-in-Chief, Western Theatre. On paper, von Rundstedt commanded all of the *Wehrmacht* forces in Western Europe, although this control was mostly operational.

*Panzer Lehr* was back from its part in *Margarethe II*, the occupation of Hungary. And the élite 1st SS and 2nd SS Panzer Divisions had returned as well, now recuperating from having fought long and hard in Russia.[1] A few smaller units in Eastern Europe were either still in transit or getting ready to move west, but most of the divisions had arrived.

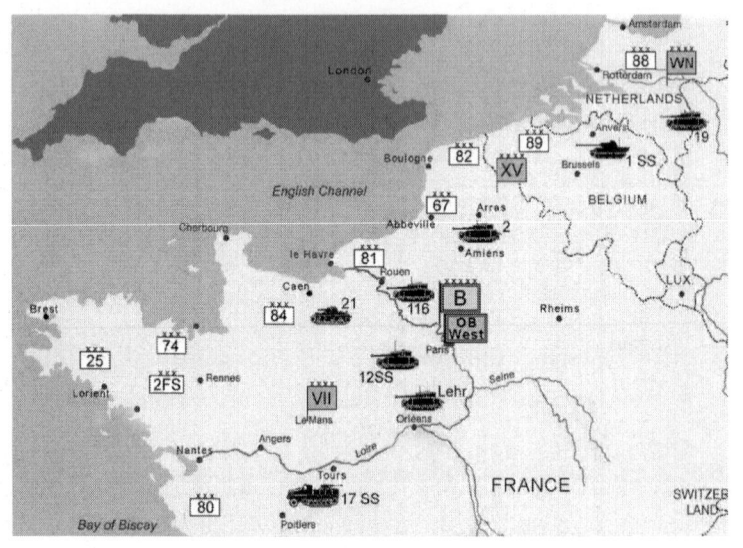

*Disposition of German Units – June 1, 1944.*

Field Marshal von Rundstedt, the overall theatre commander, now commanded (if you included some eight divisions in Holland and Belgium,[2]) about 59 divisions,[a] Of these, 34 divisions were to be considered either *'bodenstaendige'*—static units occupying coastal defenses, in training or in reserve. On the whole, they were third-rate formations with restricted movement, and they could at best only be used in limited, defensive operations. This of course, made them well-suited to defend a designated section of coastline, but severely handicapped if they had to move any considerable distance.

---

[a] While actual numbers vary, most sources show that von Rundstedt commanded between 58 to 60 divisions.

Of the remaining 24 divisions that were considered fit for combat, 11 of them could actually be considered as mobile infantry, although the phrase was one that was being stretched these days by the German High Command. The term 'mobile' could mean any sort of transport, and often referred to just horse-drawn wagons or bicycles. If a unit was lucky, it would possess a few modern motor vehicles and a wild mixture of old pre-war military vehicles, captured trucks, cars, and some motorbikes.

Two more divisions were airborne units and were trained in airborne operations to varying degrees, but of course, without any type of airdrop capability due to the weakness of the *Luftwaffe*.

On the other hand, eleven divisions were panzer formations. Three of these were élite SS units—the 1st SS, 2nd SS, and the 12th SS. A fourth unit, the 17th SS, was an oversized panzergrenadier division, with fully-mechanized, armored infantry.

Another panzer division, the rebuilt 21st, was a ghostly phoenix of its North African predecessor. Still in the process of being reorganized, it at present was equipped with so many substandard vehicles that it was considered by some to be inappropriately classified as a front-line panzer unit.[3] Even many of the new *PzKw IV*'s[a] that the division had just received were outdated. Still, it did muster at this time as an effective fighting force.

---

[a] *PanzerKampfwagen IV*. The German formal term for the Mark IV battle tank. This model with all its variations was the most produced German tank of the war. An improved version of the older *PzKw III*, it over time had in turn undergone several different modifications, or *Ausführung*. Earlier versions carried a short low velocity 75mm gun that could not compete with later Allied tanks. Later models had and increased armor protection and carried a heavier, higher velocity gun that could penetrate the armor of most American and British tanks, By 1944 though, the PzKw IV was outclassed by most of the Allied heavier armor. (Hastings, p.112)

Five more panzer units had finished their organization and training in France from the early months of 1944—the formidable *Panzer Lehr*, the 2nd Panzer, the 116th Panzer, the 9th Panzer, and the 10th Panzer. *Panzer Lehr*[a] had been formed around a cadre of knowledgeable, experienced panzer school instructors who had taught for years in training schools on panzer warfare. The last three divisions had been created out of the cadres from various other formations, including a few panzer reserve units.

The last panzer division, the 19th, was scheduled to arrive in Holland shortly. However, this division was combat weary, it too needed to be rebuilt. It was therefore not to be considered a part of the general ground order of battle, and would not be able to participate in any operations for at least a few months.[b]

All eleven panzer formations were strategically placed. Rommel and *Heeresgruppe B* directly controlled three of them. The 21st Panzer was located around the city of Caen, with each of its two panzergrenadier regiments on opposite sides of the Orne River, located near the coast. The 2nd Panzer Division and 116th Panzer Division were both on the northeast side of the Seine River, in von Salmuth's Fifteenth Army's sector, with the 2nd Panzer near Amiens, and the 116th Panzer north of Paris.[4]

Of the three divisions that were designated as High Command strategic reserves (and thus, could only be released by the Führer's direct order), the 12th SS Panzer

---

[a] Tank Demonstration or Tank Training. Created in 1943, it was made up of some of the most experienced, gifted blitzkrieg instructors and demonstration officers and non-commissioned officers in the service, and because of that, was fully-equipped and always well-supplied with the latest tanks, just like an SS panzer unit.

[b] Sources are conflicting as to the exact arrival of the 19th Panzer in Holland, but it was sometime in early June. Heavily decimated from heavy fighting in Russia, with little equipment and badly needing refitting, it would not be committed to the Normandy landing. [*Auth*].

Division (*Hitlerjugend*) and *Panzer Lehr* were inland, southwest of Paris. The third unit, the showpiece 1st SS Panzer (*Leibstandarte Adolf Hitler*[a]), was refitting up in Belgium, between Brussels and Antwerp.[5] As far as Rommel was concerned, this division was too far away to be of any good in any initial response to repelling an invasion.

The last four panzer units were allocated far down south, in *Generaloberst* Blaskowitz's *Armeegruppe G*.[b] The 11th Panzer was inland from Bordeaux, the 2nd SS Panzer was about 70 km north of Toulouse, and the 9th Panzer was located around Avignon. The 17th SS Panzergrenadier was positioned midpoint in the country, down between Poitiers and the Loire River.[6]

In addition to those 11 panzer units in the West, there was the II SS Panzer Corps, consisting of the veteran 9th SS (*Hohenstaufen*) and 10th SS (*Frundsburg*) Panzer Divisions.[c] Currently fighting in the East, it was slated to move immediately to the Western Front whenever the invasion occurred.

---

[a] Lit. 'Lifeguard;' This was the Adolf Hitler Body Guard Division, so-called because originally as a small élite SS regiment, they had been the Führer's personal guard, having sworn total allegiance to him for life.

[b] Johannes Blaskowitz's command was given the lesser status of *Armeegruppe* and not that of a *Heeresgruppe*, which was allocated more administrative resources. This was partly due to the fact that it was much smaller than its counterpart in northern France. Another reason though, was that it was a direct insult to Blaskowitz, a man whom Hitler disliked quite a bit. Besides a couple *faux pas*, Blaskowitz had officially denounced the ruthless policies of the SS in occupied Poland back in late 1939, earning the scorn of both Hitler and *SS Reichsführer* Himmler.

[c] The 9th SS Panzer Division took its title from the noble family name of 'Hohenstaufen.' This family line bred a number of German kings and emperors during the periods 1138-1208 and 1214-1254. The 10th SS was named after Georg von Frundsberg (1473 to 1528). Frundsberg was a renowned war hero who fought for the Hapsburg Monarchy in a number of wars.

Most of these divisions were still under strength, several of them very much so. This of course was testimony to the ferocity of the Soviet army, and the hard logistical problems that the Reich was facing. Nevertheless, Rommel thought, things were not too bad.

After all, a few of the panzer units were nearly at full strength. The 1st SS Panzer Division could now boast over 21,000 men. *Panzer Lehr* had nearly a full complement and was fully equipped. The battalions in the 12th SS Panzer (*Hitlerjugend*) were impressive too, made up of the cream of Germany's youth. On the other hand, many panzer units, including a few that had not yet arrived in the West, were made up of medium caliber soldiers.[7]

Regarding the construction of defensive positions along the coast, activities had slowed down some. The Allied air forces were hard at work attacking main supply lines. Complicating things was a shortage of cement, also partly due to the increased enemy bombings of the railways. The cement installation in Cherbourg had been forced to close down last month because of a lack of coal.

Regarding defensive construction, there were not enough obstacles and mines put down yet. Rommel knew that he somehow had to increase their numbers—especially if they were going to stop the enemy at the water, like he had planned. If the Allies were ever given the opportunity to establish and expand any kind of beachhead, and then somehow break out and be allowed to use their own mobility, covered by that gigantic shield of air power—well, the war would be irretrievably lost.

Where would they come? It was almost a certainty that the Allies would land along the English Channel, but in which sector? On the left? The Seventh Army there had been organized into four corps, some fifteen divisions in its ranks. The Seventh though, was not as ready as its Fifteenth Army counterpart at Calais, and was definitely the weaker brother of the two.[8]

Geographically, there were too many possible landing areas along the Channel to cover. There was the area around the Somme Estuary, Normandy, Brittany, and of course, the Pas de Calais, which was the heavy favorite location among the German Staff.

*Der Rundstedt* (as Rommel liked to call him[9]) felt that the mouth of the Loire, south of the U-boat port of St. Nazaire, was a good possibility. Some 480 kilometers long, it was thinly defended by only three divisions. Yes, they were quite vulnerable there along the Bay of Biscay. Even the unit commanders had no transportation of their own, and a lowly company commander might have to cycle all day just to cover his area of responsibility. Of course on the other hand, compared to the Channel, it would be a much farther distance for the Allies as well, and substantially harder to supply by sea.

What about Normandy? The *Kriegsmarine* had said that it had too many rocky shoals and sand bars. It was just as well. Along with a few extra battalions, there were only seven divisions to defend over 320 kilometers of coast, and four of them were static divisions.

On the Cotentin Peninsula, only four divisions were covering the area around the strategic port of Cherbourg, and that included the fortified 319th Infantry, stuck way out on the Channel Islands. It had been there since 1941.[10] The Führer had insisted early on that this island group had high political importance and had to be heavily protected. After all, this was a matter of prestige. These islands were the only British possessions that the Reich had occupied and still owned. So the well-armed 319th had been dispatched there early on. Of course, when the invasion came, unless the islands were directly assaulted, that unit would be next to useless in the overall defense scheme—stranded, and with no real means of getting back to the mainland. The men in Rommel's staff jokingly called it the "Canada" division because of its remote position,[11] and the fact that it might as well be in Canada, for all the good it would do.

So since the 319th would effectively be unusable whenever the invasion began, that left only three divisions to cover the peninsula. And if the Allies could somehow get their hands on the critical port of Cherbourg, it would give them a nice, deep-water harbor from which they could unload massive amounts of men and matériel to keep a landing supplied.

As for any local mobile reserves, the closest panzer division was the 21st, which was spread out south of Caen. Von Rundstedt had suggested that it be put further west, south of St Lô.[12] Rommel had countered by suggesting instead that the 12th SS be moved close to the Vire Estuary. No, the old Prussian wanted it kept in the strategic reserve. Terrific.

Rommel looked at his watch. Time to eat. Later this morning, he would have a meeting with Assistant Secretary Bernd with Goebbels' Ministry of Propaganda. They were going to talk about ways they could discourage the enemy when the invasion came. Then, if he had the chance, he wanted to drive up the coast to Dieppe and inspect the fortress there.[13] Dieppe and Dunkirk—both times they had thrown the Allies into the sea. Could they do it again?

---

After breakfast, Rommel was back at his study, looking over the night action summaries and latest situation reports that his aide Captain Lang had brought in. A few hundred bombers had hit some radio stations on the coast.[14] However, the Navy reported that, despite the fact that the enemy had also been hitting coastal radar stations, there were still many of both type units still operating.[15] That was good. They needed those stations to keep watch on the channel—especially northeastward, near Boulogne.

He still felt that the invasion would come near there, away from Normandy, somewhere in the Fifteenth Army sector. For one thing, Allied reconnaissance flights up there were currently outnumbering those down over the Seventh Army by a two-to-one ratio.[16] Still, he could not take any chances. Because of the high enemy air activity, all of *Heeresgruppe B* was in an alert status, although it was a low-grade one.[17]

Things seemed quiet that morning as Rommel conferred with Assistant Secretary Berndt.[a] They discussed how to psychologically influence the enemy at the actual moment of invasion. Rommel was not leaving any stone unturned.[18]

In the afternoon, Rommel took advantage of the good weather to go on the inspection trip that he had planned. He and Lang left for another look at the coast. *Oberfeldwebel* Karl Daniel,[19] his personal driver, drove them northeast to inspect the fortress at Dieppe and the shoreline covered up there by the 245th and 348th Infantry Divisions.

While examining beach defenses, he was told that the incomplete 170mm battery nearby at Ault had now twice been bombed from the air.[b] He directed that the guns be withdrawn until the concrete gun emplacements were finished.[20]

Back from his inspection late that afternoon, physically tired from stomping along the coast today and generally fatigued overall from the intense activities of the last few weeks, he received a special visitor, the military governor of Belgium and Northern France, *General der Infanterie*

---

[a] 39 year old *SS Brigadeführer* Alfred-Ingemar Berndt, Assistant Secretary of Propaganda. A strong Nazi supporter and journalist, Berndt had taken over the Propaganda Department in 1941 for Goebbels. Berndt knew Rommel quite well, having served on Rommel's command staff in North Africa as Rommel's Nazi party aide-de-camp, keeping Rommel's diary. He was a tough, bold, and when necessary, direct individual with everybody, even with his superiors (which Rommel used to his advantage whenever anything unpleasant needed to be reported to the Führer, (Irving, p.146)

[b] The battery will be hit again on June 4th by the 386th Bomb Group.

Alexander von Faulkenhausen. They settled down in Rommel's study and talked about the war. To his visiting friend, Rommel's demeanor seemed changed, reflected by just a hint of pessimism, which was uncharacteristic for him. Von Faulkenhausen concluded that the field marshal was probably just mentally and physically fatigued from the rigorous schedule that he had kept for the past few months. At any rate, he seemed to the military governor a different man than when they last saw each other in Brussels at the end of February.

The more they chatted, the more von Faulkenhausen saw how tired the field marshal was. With a possible massive invasion looming near, Rommel, feeling the stress of the responsibility that is upon him, was no longer enthusiastic and optimistic. Rather, he seemed sadly resigned and somber about Germany's chances of coming out of this war in a relatively good condition, something the visiting general himself has been convinced of for a while now.

Von Faulkenhausen later wrote:

> *"... [W]hen I repaid the visit on June 1, 1944, at La Roche-Guyon, he had changed and wholeheartedly adopted my view."*[21]

That evening, worn out after a busy day, Rommel had the opportunity to relax at a small celebration party given by his staff. Their *Ia*[a], Hans-Georg von Tempelhoff, had been promoted to full colonel. He was now *Oberst* von Tempelhoff. They also officially welcomed into their staff a new member, a certain Major Winrich Behr. The nickname "Teddy Bear" was soon coined. They also use the opportunity to bid a heartfelt farewell to *Oberst* Heckel and a few other officers who have acted as their quartermaster staff for a while.[22]

---

[a] Operations Chief.

## Friday, June 2nd

June 2nd. The nice weather continued, with a slight, cool breeze in the air. There were still no real signs of Allied activity regarding any landing operations. Not much news came down officially from higher commands. A directive was received from *OB West,* based in turn upon a 'wish' by the Führer. It extended command powers to fortress commanders.[23] A radio broadcast gave them the gloomy news (no matter how upbeat the announcer made it sound by calling it a planned strategic withdrawal) that the main Caesar Line had been broken and the 14th Army was now in retreat. The Reich today was announcing that Rome was now declared an open city.[24] Obviously, the military situation in Italy was getting even worse, now that the Allies had broken out of their Anzio landing area. It seemed likely that Rome would soon fall.

To unwind some, Rommel spent a leisurely afternoon on a hunting *battue*[a] with about a dozen of his guests. Among them was the old *Marquis de Choisy,*[25] an acquaintance that he had made during the invasion of France in 1940.[b] Together with Rommel's dog Treff,[26] they tramped around in his woods for a few hours looking for game, but only spotted a few squirrels.[c]

---

[a] From the French word meaning "beaten." A type of hunt in which herders beat the brush in front of the hunters (bird hunting) or towards them (ground hunting).

[b] According to David Irving, after the war the Marquis (whose son had fought in the *Wehrmacht* on the Russian Front) was tried and found guilty of collaborating with the Germans. He was subsequently hanged on the orders of Charles DeGaulle. (Irving, p.503)

[c] Treff was a hound dog that the *Organization Todt* had given Rommel a month ago. The name "Treff," according to Ryan, was a common German moniker for a good hunting dog. It means "a direct hit,' or 'bull's-eye,' as in hitting the target.

Although the hunting group came up empty-handed, the occasion was not a total waste of time. They enjoyed a nice walk through the lovely French woods, and occasionally, they did take in some splendid views of the placid Seine River valley on a beautiful day. The breathtaking views were only spoiled by occasional air attacks by enemy aircraft far off in the distance on the upriver Mantes bridge crossing.[27]

## Saturday, June 3rd

Saturday was another lovely morning, although as the day progressed, the skies became partly cloudy. The temperature became a bit cooler, and the wind began picking up some.[28]

Rommel as usual arose early, went to his study, and checked the incoming reports as he always did. He scanned the action reports first. During the night, enemy bombers had hit one more radio jamming station near Dieppe. Another raid had been made on four of his coastal batteries at the Pas de Calais[29].

There were three other significant messages, all of which were disconcerting. The first was a communications intelligence report. It stated that army operational centers all over England had gone on radio silence. Rommel felt a chill go through him. In the desert, radio silence usually meant that the enemy was getting ready to attack them. But here in Western Europe, after all of this wait, it could mean anything. And anyway, a number of these periods of radio silence had come and gone over the last quarter.[30]

The ramification of this message, like the others, was probably not significant. Or was it? It was after all, better to play it safe and not take any chances—not this late in the game. So Rommel wrote out a memo to his chief of staff, *Generalleutnant* Dr. Hans Speidel, requesting that the *Luftwaffe* immediately conduct aerial reconnaissance flights over all British southern ports.[31]

The second noteworthy message was from General Erich Marcks, commanding the LXXXIV Infantry Corps in Normandy. Because of both a large percentage of unsuitable supplies being delivered and a critical lack of adequate manpower, his men had fallen behind in the construction of their coastal defenses.[32] Marcks now estimated that the defensive construction program in his zone was so far only about half-complete.[33]

In addition, Marcks had copied Rommel on a message he had sent to *OB West*, requesting eight to ten small trains be put at his disposal to speed up the placement of casements in his coastal defenses.[34] Rommel smirked. Not much chance on getting those trains from the old man, especially since the Allied air forces had been attacking them steadily over the last few months.

Rommel thought about this for a bit, and then wrote out another memo for his staff. *Heeresgruppe B* was to send a request to *OB West* about all special construction undertakings and supply shipments. Those that were slated for coastal defense were hereafter to be given the highest priority.[35]

The third significant message was from the *Luftwaffe*. It reported that Allied aerial reconnaissance over France had increased the last few days. The enemy was getting quite nosy for some reason.[36] He wrote out another memo to Speidel to contact the *Luftwaffe* (again) and ask them to get some new aerial photos of the ports in southern England.

He read a copy of orders from *OKW*[a] via *OB West*, informing him that the 19th *Luftwaffe* Field Division,[b] now renamed the *19. Luftwaffe Sturm Division*, was going to be transferred out of Belgium. It was slated to travel southward,

---

[a] *Oberkommando der Wehrmacht*—The German Combined Supreme Command of all the Armed Forces.

[b] The idea for these unique units began in December 1941, when the situation on the Eastern Front had first become "critical" and manpower shortages to fill Army divisions began. In comparison, the *Luftwaffe*, shrunken down by heavy combat losses in all theatres, now had spare ground personnel that were, for all intents and purposes, 'out of a job.' Vain Reichsmarshal Göring though, rather than turn these thousands of men over to the Army, decided instead to create his own field divisions, with the *Luftwaffe* naturally retaining operational control of them. The program to establish these new units was offered to Hitler as a present on his 53rd birthday on April 20 1942. (Nafziger (2), p.141)

down through Blaskowitz's *Armeegruppe G*, and then on to Italy to fortify the crumbling line there.

He finally stood up, stretched, and left the study to go have his usual early breakfast. Lang as usual waited in the hallway to accompany him.

Later that morning, other matters later came up. A number of staff members pursued by phone some mundane subjects such as smoke candles and types of smoke-creating acids.

That morning, two army generals from the *HWaA*[a] came and promised Rommel that the manufacture of those multiple rocket launchers that he recently saw demonstrated by Major Becker's men in the 21st Panzer Division would be on schedule.[37]

There was a new message from the central SS intelligence branch in Berlin. The SS was now the army's main intelligence source since the SS had taken over the duties of the *Abwehr*.[b] The message reported a radio interception. The first verse of a Verlaine poem had been picked up:

---

[a] *Heereswaffenamt*, the Armaments Office of the German Army. The two generals were its director, *General der Artillerie* Emil Leeb, and Operations Coordinator, *Generalleutnant* Erich Schneider.

[b] In early 1944, Hitler became furious at Admiral Canaris and the dismal performance of his *Abwehr* (the German army counterintelligence branch) in the war, especially recently in its complete failure to predict the Allied landings in Italy, first at Salerno in September, and then at Anzio on January 22nd. Already distrustful of Canaris and goaded by *Reichsführer* Himmler (who saw Canaris as a direct competitor to his own SS intelligence organization), Hitler decided to dismiss Canaris and put the Army's counterintelligence branch under the auspices of the SS. He ordered its operations closed down, and its functions were greedily taken over by its counterpart branch in the SS, the *Geheimdienst*, under *SS Oberführer* Walter Schellenberg. Canaris himself, a suspected anti-Hitler conspirator, was placed under house arrest (He was eventually executed in early April, 1945). As many predicted (especially in the German Army), the Reich's counterintelligence capabilities declined even further after that.

*"Les sanglots longs des violons de l'automne."*[a]

The message concluded that, based upon past intelligence analysis, the invasion might be inspected within the next two or three weeks.[38] Maybe the low tide/full moon period of the fifth-sixth-seventh. On the other hand, Dönitz's naval headquarters had dismissed the Verlaine interception as possibly part of an enemy exercise.[39] So many variables...

Thinking about it, Rommel requested that just in case, the *Luftwaffe* should lay some *Blitzsperren*[b] in both approach channels around the Isle of Wight. Unfortunately, between the *Luftwaffe's* lethargy and the inadequacy in the West at this time, (in stark contrast to the full preparedness of the Allies), this request was probably not going to happen.[c]

Fortified by a forecasted storm coming their way, Rommel was thankful that a that a possible Allied landing in the low tide/good moon period for the period of June 4th-to-June 7th was now probably just an academic question, and for that, he was considerably relieved.

A few other last minute items were attended. Minor details that probably seemed to melt away whenever he thought about going home. He was restless—looking forward to his trip. But first he was going to Paris today.

---

[a] "The long sobs of the violins of autumn."

[b] 'Lightning fields.' Minefields that were to be laid by all available vessels as soon as the invasion was impending. (Wilson, p.160, Stillwell, p.37)

[c] At the end of May, *Luftflotte 3* only had on the books some 900 aircraft, of which only about 650 were actually deemed operational. General Kammhuber's *Luftflotte 5* in Norway had less than 200 serviceable aircraft (Hooton, p.325).

Early that afternoon, Rommel walked out of the château and climbed into the right front seat of his Horch[a], his customary seat. Daniel started the car, and they drove off to Paris.[40]

As they came into the bustling capital, they turned south and headed for *OB West,* located in the western suburb of St-Germain-en-Laye. There Rommel formally called upon Field Marshal von Rundstedt [41]at his villa. The quarters were located up a slope hundred yards or so from the massive *OB West* command bunker, which had been constructed in 1943 and was half-buried in the hill.[42] Sitting down over coffee, they chatted pleasantly. With them was *General der Infanterie* Günther Blumentritt, Field Marshal von Rundstedt's trusted chief of staff. They all sat in comfortable chairs and discussed the status of the defenses along the coast, some supply problem areas, and the upcoming bad weather. It was certainly a change from the good weather conditions of May. Rommel confessed his surprise that the Allies had not taken advantage of it. Von Rundstedt told him to be grateful that they had not.

Rommel then formally requested to go on leave in Germany from June 5th to the 8th. His request was of course no surprise to von Rundstedt.[b] They had already talked by phone about his taking time off a few days before. This was

---

[a] Rommel's vehicle of choice was a shiny black Horch 770K Tourenwagen convertible.

[b] Rommel had already mentioned the idea about taking a few days off to Jodl twice before by phone. Initially, he had suggested that he leave whenever circumstances permitted, to call on the Führer at Obersaltzburg and update him on the situation in the West. In a second conversation, he had reiterated the suggestion, and then had asked Jodl if he could coordinate this with a stopover at his home in Herrlingen, to celebrate his wife's birthday. Jodl had agreed, and had told him to just drive straight from there the next day to Berchtesgaden. Jodl tentatively set their conference up for June 7th. (CRC26-8) Rommel had then spoken by phone about the idea to von Rundstedt, who was agreeable to the idea. So Rommel's request was not new, but merely official formality.

merely the official formality. Von Rundstedt gave him permission. Besides, the 'Boy Marshal,' as he liked to call him in private,[43] looked like he needed the time off.[44]

They conversed for a while longer. Minor details. A panzer battalion from *Panzer Lehr* was going to be fitted with Panther tanks and sent to the Eastern Front. Enemy bombing of their transportation lines continued. Tactical enemy units across the Channel had gone on radio silence...[45]

Von Rundstedt told Rommel that he too was taking advantage of the bad weather. He had scheduled an inspection trip for Western France and was taking along his son. The itinerary had been radioed to *OKW* that day. He mentioned that his inspection would include a couple of their Russian *Östtruppen*, and they smiled at the thought. That would be an interesting experience.[46]

The two field marshals were soon joined by a visit from *General der Panzertruppe* Hans Cramer. He had been the last commander of Rommel's Afrika Korps before it had capitulated in Tunisia in 1943. Like his men, he had been taken prisoner by the British in May.[47]

Rommel and von Rundstedt listened in fascination as Cramer told his story. As a prisoner of war, he had taken ill with severe asthma and had decided to fake a bad lung condition to the enemy. Incredibly, the ruse had worked, and he had just been expatriated back to Germany through a skillful plan worked out by the Red Cross.

Cramer recounted that on the way to the harbor where he was to board a ship for home, he had been driven through what he thought was southeast England. Cramer had carefully taken a mental note of the images he had seen along the route. Unit headquarters, transports docked, military signposts all became a wealth of information. He also overheard a number of casual remarks, some seemingly innocuous to the speakers, and most not meant for him to hear.[48]

Cramer had later been allowed to board a neutral ship and sail back to Germany.[a]

After having been debriefed by *OKW*, he had rested for a few days, before coming to France to report his story to the two field marshals. From what he had seen, he concluded, he was convinced that the invasion would hit somewhere either below Calais or near the Somme Estuary, the latter of which just happened to be Rommel's pet theory.[49]

Cramer did add that it might have been a set up, but he believed that it was not.

Rommel finally bid his leave. They said their goodbyes, with both von Rundstedt and Blumentritt sincerely wishing Rommel a safe trip and a pleasant time while at home.

As Rommel started to walk out, he looked over at von Rundstedt and Blumentritt and addressed the possibility of a landing once more. "There's not even going to BE an invasion," he said drolly. "And if there is, then they won't even get off the beaches!"

Rommel piled back into his black Horch and set off for downtown Paris, intent on buying those birthday shoes for Lucie. In an enjoyable afternoon shopping spree he ended up purchasing a beautiful pair of handmade gray suede leather shoes—size 5-1/2, just like she had told him.[50]

---

[a] Cramer could only surmise, but he had indeed been set up by Allied Intelligence. His tour had been a carefully-staged drama, enacted solely for his benefit. Town signposts, arrows pointing the direction to fictitious military headquarters and units, and prepared scripts of off-the-wall 'remarks' were all rehearsed for him to see and to overhear. True to form, Cramer, sailing to Germany on the Swedish ship *Gripsholm*, went directly to Berlin, where he arrived on May 23rd. There he briefed OKW on what he had seen and heard, oversizing the Allied ground forces in the process - just as the Allied planners hoped he would. From there, Cramer had traveled to *OB West* to brief von Rundstedt and Rommel. (Carrell, p.16, and Irving, p.423)

On the trip back to La Roche-Guyon, he had time to think. He was of course, going home to Herrlingen[a] for Lucie's 50th birthday. After all, he had not been home for months, and this trip had been planned for some time. The impending storm approaching the Channel, coupled to the fact that the Allies seemed to be starting to get ready for something big, just confirmed the fact that this was the right time to go—probably the last chance he would have before the invasion began and all hell broke loose.

Besides, he needed a break. The pressure on him to get things ready in time had been enormous. The suspense of the Allies coming at any day, coupled to his feverish schedule, so many shortages, so many disorganized units, so much red tape—it had all taken its toll on his nerves these last few months. He had been especially tense during those good weather periods in May. He had only allowed himself to reflect the high level of stress to his Lucie in the many letters that he had written home. He was bushed, and he knew that he looked it. He had seen it in the surprised look in Blumentritt's face when he had walked into *OB West*.[51] The chief of staff had immediately noted his condition.[b]

He now looked out the car window at the passing French landscape, noting an occasional field or farmhouse. Yes, the timing for his leave seemed good. The latest weather reports confirmed that a storm front was almost upon them, so an enemy landing would be exceedingly more difficult harder. Nor were the tides right. They were scheduled around the 5th and 6th to be low in the morning. Estimates from Supreme Headquarters (*OKW*) had stated

---

[a] In the early 1970s, the town of Herrlingen, along with those of Arnegg, Bermaringen, Dietingen, Lautern, Markbronn, Weidach and Wippingen, were merged into the newly-formed municipality of Blaustein.

[b] Blumentritt later wrote in his diary that Rommel seemed "tired and tense... a man who needed to be home for a few days with his family."

that this time period would definitely not be suitable for any sort of major landing.

The *Luftwaffe's* meteorological staff felt (as Rommel had read enough times) that the assault troops would have to travel hundreds of yards further across a wider exposed beach to reach the German positions. This longer distance would naturally result in many more casualties, especially along the more fortified beach areas. It was upon this premise that most of the initial Atlantic Wall obstacles and mine barriers had been planned, laid out and positioned.[52]

Based upon these assumptions, Rommel's units had so far only worked on the high and mid-tide belts. They were well along in completion. The two low tide belts on the other hand, were definitely not. Granted, they would be easier to put in, even in spite of supply shortages; but his men in most cases not had a chance to start on them. Because of time constraints, most sectors had only been able to install the high tide and mid-tide belts, for a total of half a million offshore obstacles, and even these two belts in many places were not yet done.[53]

Even so, his men had been working hard for months, and at an unaccustomed pace. *Generaloberst* Hans Von Salmuth, commanding the Fifteenth Army, had early on in the year complained to him about this, grumbling that his men were so busy on constructing barriers that they were not getting proper training and were exhausted from the work. Rommel had shot back, "My dear von Salmuth, which would your troops rather be—exhausted, or dead?"[54] General von Salmuth had finally, grudgingly conceded to his orders and had stepped up the pace on the defenses.

Now that time was running out, Rommel was realizing that he might not have been concerned enough about the incomplete low tide belts.[55] He had thought on and off about this. Despite a talk with Staubwasser[a] they had the other

---

[a] *Oberst* Anton Staubwasser, the army group's *Ic* (Intelligence Chief). He *(Cont.)*

evening about tides, and the enemy's propensity sometimes for doing the unexpected, he still knew in his heart that the logical time to land was at high tide—close-in to the shore.

Granted, a low tide landing would render many of his present obstacles as just navigational nuisances against incoming landing craft, even though they would impede some vehicular movement in exposed positions. However, much more terrain was exposed at low tide. That would allow his coastal troops a much longer time period to fire at the invaders coming ashore. And an extra minute or two exposed to concentrated automatic fire could be devastating. With any luck, depending upon the location and time of the landing, the enemy might never make it ashore at all.

He sat back in the Horch and concentrated. Yes, the extra time would let his men fire more shells at the enemy; but there was, he acknowledged uneasily, that drawback to partially offset this—a point which many German staff officers failed to understand or fully appreciate. A landing at low tide would allow the assault force to more easily avoid and better dispose of the impeding high tide beach obstacles that would be exposed. Low tide might also allow the enemy to bring in his heavier equipment a little faster,[56] and with less difficulty.[a]

The big question was, would it be worth getting shot at for a longer period of time? He surely did not think so. Again, it all depended upon how willing the enemy was to take heavier casualties, how well that area of beach was defended, and how effective the enemy naval and air units could take the defensive positions out before the landing. However, most of the beach areas now had formidable resistance points. No, Rommel was pretty sure that they

---

had come from *Fremde Heere West* (Foreign Armies West), the intelligence branch of the Army High Command, tjat analyzed the Allied ground order of battle, the main intelligence source for lower commands. He was considered by most to be an expert on the British Army.

[a] Exactly what Eisenhower, Bradley, and Montgomery had concluded.

would come in at high or at least mid-tide. Besides, they had done that before in Italy.

As far as strategy, Rommel was adamant about his at-the-water's-edge theory. He had stressed it endlessly. That was why he had placed the 21st Panzer just south of Caen—to counter any assault along the Normandy coast. If the enemy landed in their area, they would be in excellent position to counterattack immediately. To make sure that the unit understood this, he had given the 21st Panzer a battle order back in May. It stated that the momentary weakness of the enemy right after a landing should be utilized for an automatic counterattack. They had to be like firemen, poised to jump to the scene of a blaze at a moment's notice, no matter what.

Those nagging doubts about the upcoming low-tide-at-dawn periods (of which one was coming up in two days) persisted as he rode back to his headquarters. What if he were wrong this time? The Allies had a wealth of equipment. What if they did decide to come ashore at low tide, and land a good part of their own armor first? How could his men adequately neutralize enemy tanks on the beaches? Many of his batteries would be knocked out early.

He had to hope that he was right this time. Of course, if the weather turned bad, this all would be a mute point. The Allies would have to wait. And that seemed to be what was happening. Still, he felt somewhat leery about leaving the front at this time, partly because he was beginning to feel in his heart that the Allies just might trip him up on this tide thing. He could be wrong about them landing near high tide.

This possibility continued to bother him. When he arrived at La Roche-Guyon, he got together with Speidel and gave him a summation of his trip. He then went to his study and drafted out a formal instruction. It stated that the Allies had conducted several invasion maneuvers at low tide, and that therefore, to cover this contingency, a rush program to push the anti-invasion obstacles down to low tide as well was to be started immediately, completion date to be June 20th.[57]

# I. June 1st through the 3rd — Rommel's Fateful Trip Home

That made him feel somewhat better. While his men might not be able to reach that target date, at least they would understand that there was a matter of urgency here. That is, if the Allies gave him the chance.[58]

His need for additional time was also reflected in the anti-airborne obstacle program. He wanted to take more captured surplus, odd-caliber artillery shells and install them on the tips of those stakes that had been jabbed into sections of open fields behind the beaches in Normandy. He had pleaded with the High Command for some more of these spare obsolete shells or mines—any kind of explosive device to attach to the end of each wooden spear of his `asparagus,' as the men had nicknamed it. Supreme Command had as usual dragged their feet to the point of causing madness, but a number of spare shells had eventually been delivered. In addition, yesterday, a shipment of captured French mines had finally arrived in the area. All right—now all they had to do was to get them over to LXXXIV Corps, and to install them onto the stakes.

That was about it. He had done all that he could for now. Weather forecasts called for a long storm, so he was indeed going home to visit his wife for her birthday. His instincts told him that this would be the last rest he would get before the balloon went up. All the more reason to ask Hitler personally for those extra two panzer divisions for the coast. Even though he still felt that the landing would be around the Somme Estuary, once he beefed up the Normandy area, he would feel better.

Rommel noted this in his diary late on June 3rd:

> *"The most pressing problem was to speak to the Führer personally on the Obersalzberg, convey to him the extent of the manpower and material inferiority we would suffer in the event of a landing, and request dispatch of two further panzer*

# Rommel's Fateful Trip Home    I. June 1st through the 3rd

*divisions, a Flak Corps, and a Nebelwerfer brigade to Normandy...*"[59]

Now, if only the enemy would wait just a few weeks more.[60] It began to seem like they just might...

---

*At about 9:30 p.m., the BBC broadcast the first line of the Verlaine poem, signaling that the invasion would not be far off.[a]*

*A good part of the Allied invasion fleet was by now either in the heavy seas of the Channel or in the process of leaving one of some two dozen English harbors. Many vessels had been at sea for days now. Others awaited their turn to depart.*

*The weather was rough and seemed to be getting worse. SHAEF[b] Supreme Commander General Dwight D. Eisenhower met with his command staff to determine the status of the operation. His chief meteorologist[c], told them that weather conditions in the channel would be too stormy to permit a landing on the 5th. The fleet would have to be recalled.*

*Eisenhower, a stern look of concentration on his face, sat immobile, weighing his options. He finally decided to put off*

---

[a] According to most authoritative sources, the Verlaine code was in truth only targeted for one Resistance command net, which was operating just south of the city of Orléans. The *Abwehr*, not knowing specifically who the two-part message was for, misunderstood it to be a general call to all the Resistance units in France. Even so, they were still correct in concluding that its transmission did tie in to the timing of the invasion itself. Therefore, whoever the message was directed to was in the end, an irrelevant matter if the coded implication was correct.

[b] Supreme Headquarters, Allied Expeditionary Force—The Allied top command in Europe.

[c] Group Captain J. M. Stagg, RAF.

I. June 1st through the 3rd        Rommel's Fateful Trip Home

*his decision for just a few hours, in hopes that the weather somehow would let up.* [61]

# II. June 4th—The Trip Home
"Gentlemen, here I go."

*It was the early morning hours of Sunday, June 4th. A fierce storm continued to rage across the English Channel. The Allied invasion fleet plodded through howling winds and surging waters in various areas off the English coast, struggling to make headway.*

*Eisenhower again met with his command staff around 4:30 a.m. (BDST).[a] They were told that the weather was still too rough for a landing; the invasion had to be postponed, at least until weather conditions improved. The SHAEF commander could either delay the assault for a day, and hope for a break in the weather, or he could move back the invasion date two weeks to the next period of low tides at dawn,[62] and pray that the weather would be better at that time.*

*Some forty-five minute later,[63] after more discussions, Eisenhower made his decision. He reluctantly elected to postpone the landings for 24 hours, again hoping for a break in the weather.[64] Immediately, the codeword `Ripcord 24'*

---

[a] British Double Summer Time. This time practice was set two hours later than Greenwich Mean Time (today called Zulu Time). It was also an hour later than the time in Occupied-France, which was on German Central Time (**GCT**). The Germans though, were on summer time as well. Times given in the majority of almost all D-Day accounts are understandably intermixed. This of course has caused a good deal of confusion for the researcher, as well as the reader. Most English and American documents of the Allied activities are given in BDST, although some personal Allied accounts are interestingly given in GMT. Most of the German and French accounts or documents are given in GCT, an hour behind the British. I have tried to reconcile the many time accounts here. All times given are in GCT, unless otherwise noted.

*was radioed to the Allied fleet, now approaching the French coast in the grueling seas. D-Day had been delayed for at least a day.*

*Most of the few thousand ships already at sea immediately began to turn back. Inevitably, as things often happen in complex operations, even with the best of plans, some units did not receive the recall, despite the fact that it was repeated enough so that everyone would get notified. One force of minesweepers was only 35 miles from the beaches when it finally got the word and changed course.[65] Another contingent, after hours of frantic, unsuccessful attempts to signal them, finally, grudgingly, turned back for England, a scant 26 miles from the invasion coast.[66]*

*Although the force's approach was picked up by at least one German radar station and reported to their naval headquarters in Cherbourg, when the contacts began moving northward again and finally got lost in England's ground interference,[67] the German radar crews lost interest in the contacts, and the report was filed as routine.[68]*

*The Allies were lucky.*

---

At La Roche-Guyon, dawn of Sunday, June 4th was gray and misty.[69] The town was still wet in the aftermath of the brutal storm that had come across the channel. Torrents of rain and heavy winds had raged across a dry, baked land.[70] The worst of the storm's first phase for now had abated inland, and in the gray fog, the château of *Heeresgruppe B* eerily loomed out of the mist like a giant leviathan.[71]

The road leading towards the château was as usual devoid of traffic, more so because it was Sunday. The countryside was deserted, except for the sentries in their camouflaged capes dotted throughout the area.[72]

Rommel sat in his study behind his huge, priceless desk,[73] with its solitary lamp providing the only light in the room. It was early, and he was alone. He had been up since 3 a.m., listening to the early morning sounds outside. It had still been raining while he was in the bathroom,[74] though the rain had now subsided somewhat.[75]

He put down the report he had been reading and stood up, rubbing his eyes. He yawned, stretched his arms, and winced as a dull pain ran through his lower back. His lumbago[a] was acting up again.[76] He looked down and glanced at his watch. It was after 5 a.m.

He wandered over to the French window on his left. He glanced out through the rain rivulets dripping down the glass pane. Peering into the gloom of the early morning, he made out what was left of his rose garden on the terrace. Rommel sighed softly. His lovely roses had suffered badly in last night's storm, and now pedals, twigs, and broken plants lay haphazardly all over the veranda.[77]

And yet, as he looked up at the overcast sky, the continued bad weather was overall for him a good thing. It was his ally. It meant no invasion for this particular low-tide period. So it looked like his trip home for Lucie's birthday and then down to Hitler's mountain retreat, the Berghof, to see Hitler was still on.[78] He tensed a bit. To see the Führer once again...

He walked back to his desk and sat down. He was tired. Well, he was going home in a little while.[b] That would help.

---

[a] A chronic, aching lower back pain (lumbar region), common for people in their middle ages. Possible causes are strained back muscles, a slipped disc, arthritis and displaced vertebrae.

[b] The at times surprising controversy as to when Rommel left for home has pretty much been settled. The most authoritative writers of the invasion—Ruge, Irving, Ryan, Fraser, Reuth, Toland (*Adolf Hitler*, p.890)—put his departure date at June 4th. Several have stated that it was June 5th, including, surprisingly, Rommel's own chief of staff, Hans Speidel (*Invasion 1944*). Other authors simply leave the date out (such as pioneer biographer Desmond Young in *The Desert Fox*, and Harrison in his exhaustive *Cross Channel Attack*). However, most eyewitnesses (Lang, Tempelhoff, Ruge, and Rommel's own wife and son), as well as *(Cont.)*

As usual, he had slept no more than four or five hours.[79] The upcoming trip was part of the reason. Mostly though, it was the continued stress of last minute preparations, while having to stay ready for an invasion that could come at any time. And there was so much at stake. The fate of Germany rested on his shoulders. Hitler had said so.[80] A successful Allied invasion in France now would irrevocably cost Germany the war, no matter how many secret weapons their scientists created.[81]

Ah, as if they could win.

Oh, he had known since North Africa that they could not really win the war. But if the Americans and British ever got a toehold on the European continent, Germany would irrevocably lose any chance of ending the war with them separately by a negotiated peace. And if that happened, and if Hitler could not be persuaded to step down from office, they would inevitably be destroyed as a country. Their already-damaged cities would be demolished, their industries burnt to the ground—just like in Russia.

Yes, a great deal was indeed riding on him. He also knew that, as always, he would give it his best effort whenever the invasion came. Until then, he just wanted some time off. And today he was going home.

He had decided that there was to be no fanfare on this trip. He had told Lang that they would have no escorts on the road. Their route and their itinerary were to be secret. No one was to know that they were coming through. It was not just a matter of a need for security (Between the complete Allied air supremacy and the Underground, the threat was indeed real). It was also one for obscurity. Too many local commanders would turn out to shake his hand, or to get him to inspect their 'élite' guard.

---

the Army Group B War Diary, confirm that his departure date was indeed on the 4th.

Rommel did not want to waste his precious leave on that. For a change, he wanted no public accolades, no brass bands—not this time. The weather was bad, and he was fatigued. So he was going to take a quick trip home. With any luck, he would make it there by early evening. A couple days rest, then a short hop down to the Berghof. One last appeal to Hitler to give him the 12th SS to put near the coast. And he was going to ask for a rocket brigade. Both were for the Normandy area.[82]

---

Down the hallway in the office of the army group's chief of staff, sat a German army captain wearing spectacles. He was about 1.8 meters tall, and weighed a trim 72 kilograms.[a] A blue-eyed, clean-shaven, handsome bachelor, he had sandy-colored hair and a square jaw that the ladies seemed to like. This was Field Marshal Rommel's aide, 36-year old Captain Hellmuth Lang.[83] He was at the moment looking over the morning reports.

Lang had replaced one-eyed Lieutenant Hammermann as Rommel's aide back in early February.[84] Hitler's army adjutant, General Schmundt,[b] had insisted at the time that Hammermann's replacement be someone of higher rank and stature than a mere lieutenant. Rommel in turn had stipulated that if this was to be the case, that the replacement be at least a major in rank, a fellow Swabian, somewhat decorated, and a panzer officer. Lang, an easy-mannered fellow, although only a captain, fit the bill in every other way. A prewar acquaintance of the field marshal's as a panzer instructor, he had distinguished himself in Russia, earning himself the Knight's Cross. And being from the town of Schwäbisch-

---

[a] About 5'11" and 180 lbs.

[b] Schmundt was also the Chief of Personnel for the German Army.

Gemünd, east of Stuttgart in Rommel's own Swabia, had been the last point in earning him the position.[85]

Today, they were going on leave. Hopefully they would leave the château by seven. Besides Lang and the field marshal would be the Operations Chief *Oberst* von Tempelhoff.[86] They would be traveling in a convoy of two cars. No flying home this time. The Führer had insisted that if general officers wanted to fly anywhere, they had to ride in an aircraft with at least three engines, and be accompanied by an adequate fighter escort. Rommel did not want to tie up so many critical aircraft—and anyway, he preferred to travel by car.[87]

Lang was going to ride with Rommel and their driver, Corporal Daniel. The cultured newly-promoted von Tempelhoff, on his way home to see his wife in Bavaria, would ride in the second vehicle,[88] driven by a sergeant. As the field marshal had ordered, their leave remained secret. Lang made sure that no one had been informed of their trip, much less their itinerary. In addition, Rommel's Horch would not be flying his honorary field marshal's banner on the front bumper. And he had insisted that the two cars were to have no escort to attract attention.[89]

These measures worried Lang, because they would be in real trouble if they had motor problems or were in any kind of accident. And what if, God forbid, they were ambushed along the road by the Resistance? True, they each carried a pistol, including the field marshal.[90] But that would not be enough firepower against any kind of coordinated terrorist attack.

Well, no matter. That was a chance they would have to take. Besides, they were going to travel light and fast. The field marshal wanted to dispense with all of the protocol and ceremony that seemed to confront him everywhere he went because of his rank and popularity. After all, he wasn't just a field marshal—he was *der Wüstenfuchs*, one of the greatest heroes of the German people.

Actually, it was a bit more than that. True, he was very popular, both with the *Wehrmacht* and the German people. But more importantly, despite their occasional differences, he was still one of Hitler's 'fair-haired boys'. And anyway, the public had not been told of the couple of times when Rommel had fallen out of favor. That would have hurt morale, so vitally important at this time. Besides, Lang believed, as did most people, that he was the Third Reich's last hope for an honorable victory.

As usual, Lang had the day before considered what they would take for lunch along the way. Usually the field marshal ate little when on the road. The aide had settled this morning on bringing a thermos of consommé and some sandwiches. Chances were that taking the food along would just be a futile gesture. As was so often the case, the field marshal probably would either forget about lunch or not be hungry.[91]

Lang stood up and walked out of Speidel's office with the morning message traffic. Turning left, he walked down the hallway of the elegant château. He checked the time. It was about five minutes before five. The noise level from the surrounding offices grew louder—evidence that the staff of Army Group B was beginning its day, as it usually did around now. Reports had started to come in and new ones had to go out. New assessments had to be evaluated, and phone calls had to be made.

Lang stopped at the end of the corridor and stood before the huge door leading to the field marshal's study. He knocked softly, then without waiting for any acknowledgment, turned the handle and discreetly walked in.[92]

The field marshal was sitting at his desk, absorbed in his papers and did not look up. Lang stood there quietly, courteously, and waited.

Finally, Rommel sensed his presence and glanced up at him. "Morning, Lang," he said amiably.

"Good morning, *Feldmarschall*," Lang replied respectfully. "The reports."[93]

He handed the papers to the field marshal, then turned and left the room, quietly closing the huge door behind. He stood in the hall, waiting as usual for the field marshal to go through the reports, so that they could go to breakfast.

---

Rommel glanced at the latest reports, just delivered by Lang. They did not disclose much that was new or significant. There was an increase in Resistance radio message traffic. The predicted low tide periods were summarized. Moderate air activity. There had been a number of bombings last night along the Pas de Calais, and in the Seventh Army area.[94]

One release was disconcerting. As he had read yesterday, the Allied army-level operational centers across the Channel were continuing their ominous radio silence. This condition had persisted for a few days now. Although these periods had come and gone before, this one for was starting to really worry him. And yet, with a storm approaching, this scheme had to be a feint.[95]

So why would Eisenhower bother with it, if this ploy was so clearly a fake one? Allied intelligence was not that dumb. What else could it mean, then? Normally radio silence was used either as a ruse, or as the prelude to a real operation. Perhaps even the long-awaited invasion.

But in stormy weather? Hardly. Why make things so for your men? And yet, the tactic was working on his already-overworked nerves. He could not be sure that the enemy was not getting ready for something.

A copy of his latest Army Group B weekly estimate to *OB West*, also in front of him, reflected this thought. It stated that the enemy had achieved a "high degree of readiness," with an "increased volume of messages going to the French resistance." Still, his report stated that these conditions were nothing new, and by themselves, did not necessarily indicate that the invasion would be forthcoming. Rommel concluded with "according to past experience this is not indicative that an invasion is imminent."[96] Well, that was surely sticking his neck out.

He turned his attention to the *Luftwaffe* 5 a.m. meteorological report. It started off by stating that there was at present a storm in the Channel area. Rommel grunted softly. He did not need see a report to know THAT. The winds last night had made their presence known to him a number of times, and his poor roses that morning gave testimony to the strength of the gusts.

He read on. The German forecasters predicted that bad weather would continue for at least another three or four days, with heavy swells and rain over the entire English Channel. The winds, now between Force 5 or 6, were forecast to go up to Force 6 at the Pas de Calais, and up to Force 7 at Cherbourg,[97] with gales in the Channel averaging 48 km/hr. The heavy cloud base was low—275 to 550 meters—and the storm in the channel was producing waves over two meters high,[98] with a rough sea that was to probably going to continue the next day at Force 4 or 5. It was still raining or drizzling in some places inland. Not a good time for an invasion, by any means.[99]

He glanced at the *Kriegsmarine* report. It too mentioned the stormy seas in the Channel, and that it would be at least two weeks before meteorological conditions and the tides were again right for an invasion.[100]

The *Luftwaffe* reports detailed the intensive nightly bombings, most of them in the Calais area. They were now becoming a regular occurrence. These air raids further reinforced the idea that the invasion would come up there. Well, if it did, his men would be ready for them.[101]

In the meantime, it was raining, so he was going on leave. This was an opportune time to take it, with the storm and all. The good weather of May had surprisingly not produced the expected invasion. His instincts told him it would not come for at least another fortnight. He was pretty sure now that it would be timed with the Russian summer offensive, and that could not begin for another few weeks yet—until Poland's late thaw came, as it usually did, in the last half of June.

Anyway, he had to see the Führer as soon as possible—in person, and hopefully in private. It was the only way he could persuade him that the Atlantic Wall was short of supplies and men. They needed more mines, rocket launchers, more infantry, and better cooperation from the navy and air force. Most of all, he needed to get control of the massive OKW panzer reserves, so that he could station them closer to the front and be able to commit them much quicker. And maybe they could chat about the future. That was a special subject that Rommel might try to ease into the conversation.

There was a decent chance that Hitler would listen to him, at least about the panzers and the rocket brigade. Rommel was once again in good standing, and, after all, the last man who gets in to see the Führer often got his way. How often had he said that? Well, this time he intended to be that last man. He needed those panzers near the coast.[102] Especially the 12th SS, which he was going to reposition just north of St. Lô…

---

A few minutes after having given the field marshal the latest reports, Lang was standing patiently in the hallway, waiting for him to finish going over them.[103] Lang wondered once again if they were still leaving today. Rain or not, it was, after all, a bad time to be going home.

For one thing, the field marshal was very busy these days. More importantly though, Spring was ending. The invasion could come any day now, and beach defenses, although they were coming along nicely, were still far from being finished yet, especially in the Seventh Army sector. The Allied bombings of the railroads and the many bridges over the northern French rivers had seriously slowed down the supply movement to the western coastal areas, especially lines from the northeast. Nearly all of the ten major bridges across the Loire River[104] in the central region had been taken down by bombs,[a] and as fast as they could be repaired, the enemy would hit them again.[105]

Still, all things considered, it seemed that there would not be a better time to leave for some time to come. The weather was bad, enemy activity was low (except for those *verdamnt* bombers), and the field marshal had wanted to see the Führer for a while now. Timing aside though, this trip home still created a number of concerns. Recent air activities would play a factor. Damage to roads and bridges by recent Allied bombings force might force them to make wide detours. Would they be able to travel without getting strafed? Then there was the Resistance to consider. Even well-wishing, big crowds awaiting their arrival would not just delay them, but also pose a threat to security…

He was still in thought when the door swung open, and the field marshal stepped out.

"Ah, good morning, Lang," he greeted his aide warmly, as if he were seeing him for the first time that day. "Are we ready to go?"[106]

Lang smiled and replied, "*Yawohl, Herr Feldmarschall.*" So they wandered off together to eat breakfast. It was about 6 a.m.

They walked into the dining room and were warmly greeted by the senior staff members. They sat down, and

---

[a] The Germans considered the bridges south of Normandy more critical than those to the northeast, especially the four critical ones over the Seine river. Blocks along the Seine would hinder supplies getting to the area's flank, whereas destroyed bridges across the Loire to the south, especially the three double-tracked rail lines in the city of Tours, critically held up supplies that were headed towards the front.

## II. June 4th—The Trip Home

were immediately served. The staff all began talking, and Rommel occasionally joined in with a remark or two.

Rommel took his customary place at the head of the large dining table, with his seven senior staff members in the other chairs. General Hans Speidel—*der Chef*—as usual sat next to him on one side, and Admiral Friedrich Ruge, his naval advisor, sat on the other. Along with them sat General Meise, their engineering advisor, General Gerke, who oversaw communications, and Colonel von Tempelhoff—Rommel's *Ia*.[a] Also at the table was General Staubwasser, the *Ic*, and General Lockman, the chief artillery advisor. Lang, as Rommel's aide, qualified to sit at the table, and so made the count nine.[107]

Lang noticed the slight tension in the room. They were all of course well aware of the old man's trip today, and how important it was to see Hitler. The break in the weather was giving him the chance,[108] probably the last one before the invasion began.

After breakfast was served, they got down to business. All the senior staff advisors summarized the possible problems he might come across in his visit to the Berghof. General Meise reminded him twice after some appropriate remark, "And make sure *Feldmarschall*, that you get me more mines."

They discussed the different tacks he might use with the Führer. One had to be subtle, yet persuasive. The field marshal's main goals, they summarized, were threefold—first, to convince the Führer of the seriousness of the situation in the West; second, to get the supplies that they desperately needed; and third, to tell the High Command to release the reserve panzers to them, so that they could be repositioned much closer to the coast.

---

[a] The *Ia* in a German unit was the Operations Officer. The *Ic* was the Intelligence Officer.

Rommel listened patiently to his staff as he sipped his tea and spread some honey on his buttered slice of white bread. Once in a while, he would check the time. The conversation eventually became informal. The staff members had relaxed now, and they spoke in casual tones, even though Rommel was leaving soon. He listened to them patiently, not saying much, and nodding once in a while when a good point was made, occasionally glancing at his watch.[109]

He felt a bit tense about the trip, but he stayed in good humor. He quickly finished eating and thereafter listened patiently to his staff members, looking at them as they spoke. He was not a big eater, and certainly no gourmet. On the other hand, unlike him, they were, and therefore enjoyed a nice, full breakfast.

At one point during the meal, Rommel, noting the quality of the food on the plates before him, looked down the table at his aide.

"Lang," he asked mischievously, "Do ALL the men at my headquarters get the same sort of breakfast?"

Lang smiled back at him. "*Yawohl, Feldmarschall*," he replied, "But it isn't served quite as pleasantly as this."[110] They all laughed affably.

Breakfast finally ended, and the dishes were picked up. With the critical subject of the Berghof trip having been covered, the conversation turned to less pressing matters. It was evident to Lang that Rommel was getting impatient to leave.

At 6:47 a.m., he once again looked at his watch, and suddenly announced, "Gentlemen, here I go."[a] They all got up with him, [111] filed out of the dining room, and walked down the corridor towards the main door, Rommel in the lead, his senior staff following him. Other staff members had

---

[a] According to Ryan's original notes. In his book, he changed the quote to Rommel saying "Gentlemen, I must go."

gathered to wish him well. Along the corridor and stairs were junior officers and NCOs, having awaited for a while now to get the opportunity to wish him good fortune on his trip, and to tell the Old Man *auf wiedersen*. Walking slowly down the hallway, he took the opportunity to shake their hands and murmur an occasional comment to one or another. He reached the front door and walked out with his senior staff.

Outside stood Corporal Daniel, with both doors on the right side of the beautiful, cleaned up shiny black Horch, open and waiting. Behind it was a second car for von Tempelhoff to take. He too was going home, and he would take the other vehicle on past Herrlingen to his home in Munich.[112]

Rommel though, turned to Tempelhoff and invited him to ride in the front car with him and Lang until their turnoff came.[a] Von Tempelhoff's accompanying sergeant could follow in his car behind them. The colonel accepted the invitation, and climbed into the back of the Horch.[b] Lang got in after him and closed the door.[113]

Rommel turned each of his remaining staff members and shook their hands.[114] He mentioned that there was little chance of an invasion coming now. The bad weather would make the low morning tides useless in the following days. No, Rommel was not expecting a landing now. He believed that if it was to come at all, it would be around the middle of June—sometime around the 20th, when the moon was full.[115] Anyway, the reconnaissance branches had given them no hint of landing preparations—not that there had been any significant German air reconnaissance at all to speak of recently.[116]

---

[a] Von Tempelhoff lived in Munich, to the southeast.

[b] Von Tempelhoff erroneously remembers Rommel's car as being a "gray Wunderbar." Perhaps he was referring to the second vehicle.

He then said a few parting words to Speidel.[a] Lang guessed it was some sort of "Don't-worry" speech.[117] After all, they did not expect any problems. They then shook hands gravely, and paused briefly, hand in hand. Speidel looked at his superior solemnly and said quietly, "Good luck."[118]

Rommel seemed touched. He smiled slightly, and then turned and climbed into the front seat of the Horch next to Daniel (his usual spot). He momentarily turned around to look at Lang and von Tempelhoff sitting in the back and then beamed as he raised a cardboard box with his left hand, to show them that he had not forgotten. Inside the box was Lucie's birthday present—the Parisian gray shoes that he had picked out yesterday.[119]

He turned back around and put the box back on the seat beside him. She would be so happy as she turned fifty. She would have those beautiful Parisian shoes, and he would be home. Indeed, for Lucie, June 6th would be a special day.

They were finally ready to leave. Rommel looked over at his driver and said, "We can go now, Daniel."

Daniel started the car and put it into gear.

It was about 7 a.m.[120]

---

The big, rumbling Horch started off slowly, circled around the courtyard, and rolled majestically through the main gate, followed by von Tempelhoff's car. They passed the beautiful linden trees along the drive, and entered the small village of La Roche-Guyon. There the two cars turned left onto the main road leading southeast to Paris.[121]

---

[a] Admiral Ruge wrote that Rommel had at some time recently thoroughly discussed with Speidel the measures to be taken in case of an attack. That statement could be given a critical eye, considering Speidel's actions two days later in the early morning hours of the 6th.

The trip home started out uneventfully. The four of them sat quietly and serenely admired the beautiful scenery of the French countryside as it rolled by. Occasionally, someone commented on a view.

Corporal Daniel as always drove silently. He had been with the field marshal for many months, and had taken him anywhere he wanted to go—safely, and without comment. That was one of the reasons Rommel liked him, because he was quiet and did not talk very much, which of course, gave Rommel frequent opportunities to snooze in the car. Today, as they drove along the Seine towards the capital, Rommel smiled over to him and asked pleasantly, "And how is Daniel?"[122]

The driver smiled and politely replied that he was fine. The field marshal nodded in approval. Usual small talk.

They drove along the Seine River to Paris, and from there, they took the main highway towards Châlons-sur-Marne.[123]

Rommel finally half-turned and began to talk, mainly to von Tempelhoff. He discussed a new land mine that he wanted to get a good supply of. Constructed of glass, it was virtually non-metallic, and as such would not be found by enemy mine detectors.[a] He wanted them placed in and around roads, especially intersections. Another type that they needed was in the water. It was a pressure mine. When a vessel passed over it, the detonator sensed the varying water pressure above it and would detonate, thus tearing out the ship's bottom.

Turned around, Rommel looked at von Tempelhoff. "We must have these mines," he stressed. "We just *must* have these mines."[124]

The Horch continued across France. After Châlons-sur-Marne, they drove eastward to Bar le Duc, and from there, on towards Nancy.[125]

---

[a] Same theory as used on the "Schumine 42."

Rommel inevitably began thinking of the invasion date. For some reason (the weather notwithstanding), the enemy had delayed his assault. Perhaps it would not come at all. That seemed foolish of them.

Anyway, the landing would not come for a few weeks. The weather was bad right now, and coordinating with the Russian offensive seemed likely. And most certainly the invasion would be tied to a pre-assault airborne landing. The Allies would of course want a full moon for that, and the next one would not come until June 20th.[a] On the other hand, the Allies had never initiated an invasion on a full moon before.[126]

There was even a good chance that the invasion might be put off until July, or maybe even August. A couple more months would surely make a significant difference for him. A few millions more mines planted, a few thousand offshore obstacles—and that low tide belt could be completed. That is, IF the enemy waited.

"Time," he said, "is the important thing now for us."[127]

There was some food that had been brought along. Inside a lunch basket that had been packed under Lang's direction were, among other things, a number of sandwiches. Some of them had one or two thick slices of cheese, and some of them were *würst*—fresh slices of white bread with thick layers of choice sausage between them. There was some fruit, and each of them had a box of what the men called "iron rations." Lang and von Tempelhoff snacked some as they rode. Daniel drove and did not eat. There was also some tea in a thermos. Von Tempelhoff and the field marshal each took a cup.

Rommel began a lengthy discussion with his Operations Officer about the upcoming visit with the Führer. They went

---

[a] Rommel had once told Lang, it [the invasion] is going to come at all, it will be around the middle of June, sometime around the 20th, when the moon is full."

over their objectives once more. Foremost was the need to get operational control of the reserve panzers. Once they were his to command, he would be able to move them closer to the coast, so that they could react much more quickly to a landing.[128]

He was also going to try to impress upon the Führer the seriousness of the differences between them and the enemy in the amount of equipment, and especially their lack of airpower. Relatively few high-ranking commanders had experienced first-hand, full-scale warfare against the Western Allies in the last two years. The enemy of 1940 had changed radically. Few of his fellow generals had suffered as he had from the massive airpower that the Americans and the British could wield.

Hopefully, the Führer would ask him what he might suggest. Here he intended to ask for an antiaircraft corps—there was General Wolfgang Pickert's III Flak Corps, for instance. It consisted of four flak regiments, containing a total of some 24 batteries. The corps headquarters was at Amiens;[129] but the batteries themselves were scattered about in northern France to engage bomber formations on their way into Germany.

One regiment[a] was on its way to the mouth of the Vire River in Normandy;[130] But the others were dispersed in the Somme River area. Rommel wanted to put them all in Normandy. If the invasion hit further north, *Luftwaffe* fighter units could more than take up the duties of the flak units.

And he would then press (but tactfully, and gently, oh so gently) for the Führer's assurance that the *Luftwaffe* would be committed in *en masse* once the invasion began. Rommel knew that they would be woefully outgunned in the skies,

---

[a] The 1st Flak Regiment, formerly 431st (Nafziger, p.427), left Trouville June 3rd, and arrived at Grandcamps at the Vire estuary the morning of June 5th.

but without their presence, ground units would be easy prey for the overwhelming Allied air presence.

---

With the field marshal gone, the empty morning seemed to drag on at La Roche-Guyon. The weather continued to be rainy for the rest of the day, as stormy westerly winds hit them periodically.[131] Despite the rain, the atmosphere at the château turned into a calm, almost holiday routine. A couple of incoming calls dealt with whether or not inland shipping should operate in the bad weather. The rainy day dragged on, and they hoped the field marshal was having an uneventful trip to his home in southern Germany.

Speidel dispatched a message to OKW, reporting that *Heeresgruppe B* might stand down its two armies during the bad weather, so that the units might get some rest after the low-grade alert they had been on for a while now. He also added that enemy air activities still indicated the Straits of Dover as the likeliest landing area.[132]

---

Rommel's motorcade rolled on uneventfully through Nancy, and in due time came into the French town of Luneville. The conversation drifted as they talked about the situation in general. Rommel, frank and unafraid, complained about the High Command staff at OKW. The presence of incompetents at such a high level and constantly influencing the Führer was bad for the war effort. 'Yes-men' like Wilhelm Keitel, and glory-hounds like Walther Warlimont were not doing anyone any good. And sometimes, the Führer's orders ended up not being carried out like they should be, but rather twisted, left half-finished, or simply ignored. Rommel turned to his audience in the back and added, "I realize that Hitler gives orders; but they're not implemented. Now how can I tell Hitler this?"[133]

Suddenly, they heard a shot. A partisan attack? They all were wearing their sidearms, although they had never used them. But with no escort...

A few seconds of travel was all they needed to realize that the Horch had a flat tire. Daniel pulled over, the second car following suit, and they all got out.

Daniel proceeded to begin on the flat, and the sergeant driving the other car assisted. The three passengers emerged from the vehicles and stretched their legs.

As the two enlisted men worked on the flat tire, the rest of them stood around, waiting, admiring the town of Luneville. A lady approached them along the walk. She had been shopping, and she carried in one hand a shopping bag. Her other hand was clutched to that of a pretty little girl walking beside her. Her daughter, of course.[134]

As the two of them approached the motorcade, they took in the scene. Suddenly the mother, noticing the field marshal, must have realized who he was, because her eyes widened in recognition. She stopped, crouched down next to the youngster, pointed up at him, and said excitedly, "*Regardez, Cherie!* There is Field Marshal Rommel!"

They all smiled, and Rommel, his worries temporarily forgotten, bent down and picked the little girl up. She stared at him with big eyes, somewhat puzzled, but nevertheless innocently warm. She then smiled at him, and he grinned back at her.

He turned to his aide and said, "You see that, Lang? They really do like me."[135]

Rommel held the child a bit longer, murmuring to that sweet face, before returning her to her mother. Then the two of them, mother and infant daughter, beamed at him once more and then walked off. The men were all heartened by the episode.

The tire finally fixed, they were off once more. Lang told them that he was glad to be moving again. He admitted that he had thought for a moment the tire noise had been a shot. After all, an assault upon their two cars would be a disaster.

Rommel laughed. He never worried about such things, even when the toured the coastal areas. He simply did not take such possibilities seriously. His luck had not held on this long for him just so that he could be bumped off by some peasants in the hills.[136]

After a while, the talk again turned towards the upcoming visit with Hitler.[137] They reviewed one more time how Rommel could best explain his well-worn opinion on why they needed full control of the panzers, and why they should be positioned near the coast. Rommel also repeated that he was going to ask for some flak units. And, he added, a rocket brigade.

"The *Nebelwerfers,*" von Tempelhoff said.

Rommel nodded. "We need them." He wanted to put them in Normandy.

What was the best tack to take in making Hitler aware of the seriousness of their dilemmas? He wondered again if he would get any of what he was asking for. Probably not.[138]

True, he was in the Führer's good graces again. But times were hard, and supplies were short. And after Rommel left the Berghof, someone undoubtedly would get to him and persuade him to change his mind. Again, the last one who saw Hitler was the one that usually got his way. Rommel frowned. That was a pet peeve of his.

Rommel's two-car convoy neared the German border. The scenic city of Strasbourg lay ahead of them. They were now talking about the war in general. It seemed like no one had anything positive to say about it. Rommel confessed that he had some doubts as to whether or not the trip would be successful. No matter what the outcome of his meeting with the Führer, the panzers would probably remain under OKW's authority—and that would put them inland, and out of reach. Rommel began talking about bad government in general, and how many things decayed under the rule of a tyrant.

Lang looked at him and asked, "*Mein Feldmarschall*, How far does a dictator have to go before somebody overthrows him?"

The car went quiet at such a bold question. Lang was embarrassed, and Rommel hesitated. True, he allowed free, unfettered speech in his company, and there was no political or SS officer in his command, like the Soviets required and many other German army headquarters carried. That was disgraceful. But this was a precarious topic. And everyone knew who they were talking about when they used terms like "dictator" and "tyrant."[139]

Rommel stared ahead at the road and said evenly, "Lang, there's no use talking about that." They were all quiet, pondering the implications of his statement, as Lang turned red. The car went on. Had he said the wrong thing?

Then Rommel turned around to face his aide. "But if you want my private opinion," he said in a low voice, "I would say this: The man who overthrows the tyrant must have three distinct capabilities."

He held up a gloved finger. "One: he must have complete and total knowledge of the military situation. And I don't mean just here," he said, indicating the western Front. "Somebody like a division commander."

A second finger came up. "Two: he must be a man who is not overthrowing the tyrant because of fanaticism, or personal ambition. He must be someone who realizes his responsibilities, not only to himself, but to his nation, and to its people."

"Three: he must be able to bring something better to his people than they've had before; Otherwise, nothing would result but complete chaos."[140] They discussed the matter a bit more.

They passed through lovely Saverne[141] and finally rode into Strasbourg at about 4 p.m., talking about how Rommel could handle Hitler. They stopped at a checkpoint and noticed an escort of vehicles sitting in the road.[142] The commander of the escort came up to the car, saw Rommel on the other side, and circled in front of the Horch. Rommel and Lang both rolled down their windows.

The captain came to attention, saluted, and said, "*Herr Generalfeldmarschall*, I have orders to escort you through the city."

Rommel glanced back at Lang, who shrugged his shoulders. No mention was made in any communiqués about them coming through—much less their exact route. No teletypes, no phone calls, no orders, no nothing.[143]

Was there a security leak somewhere? No, very unlikely. Probably someone who had spotted them in one of the towns that they had already passed through had sent word on ahead of them. It was a common thing for VIPs.

Fine. Rommel nodded approval, and the motorcade quickly joined the two cars. The vehicles moved somewhat slowly through the historic town,. The officers observed the shops and the pedestrians who would stop and stare at the vehicles. Many people waved to them and a few even cheered. Rommel just occasionally smiled and shook his head, impatient to move on.

They finally reached the other side of the city, and the escort vehicles pulled over. Rommel motioned the emerging captain of the guard over to his car, and asked Lang to pursue the security matter.

Lang rolled his window down again and, looking out at the captain standing next to the vehicle he asked, "Who did you get your orders from?"[144]

The captain, puzzled, was not sure of the question.

"How did you know that we were coming?" Lang clarified.

"Well," the man said, hesitating, "we received orders that the field marshal would pass through Strasbourg today."

Lang looked at him, thinking about that comment, when Rommel, sitting in the front, impulsively leaned toward his open window and asked, "Do you know who I am?"

The indignant captain frowned at him, looked up, and smartly came to attention, clicking his heels. Why, yes sir!" he replied proudly in classic parade ground fashion. "You are *Generalfeldmarschall* von Rundstedt!"[145]

Rommel scowled at the man as his traveling companions behind him tried very hard to repress their laughter. Corporal Daniel kept a straight face.

Looking up at the captain, the field marshal barked, "ROMMEL!" Was that a muffled snicker coming from behind him?

"Come on, Daniel," Rommel growled. "Drive on."[146]

They left the city behind them, Lang and Tempelhoff in the back, hiding their grins as the field marshal just shook his head.

They went on, soon reached Freudenstadt, Speidel's home town, and drove through it. At one point, they passed dozens of schoolchildren, who smiled and waved to his car as it passed them. Rommel smiled and remarked to his aide, "Lang, you can see that they trust me."

They eventually came into beautiful Stuttgart. There, Lang took his leave of them and, in a change of plans, took the second car so that he could have transportation.[a] The two cars left in different directions, Daniel headed for Ulm to drop off von Tempelhoff, and Lang, accompanied by the second driver, headed for his 400-year old townhouse in Schwäbisch-Gemünd.[147]

Rommel's Horch passed the turnoff for Herrlingen and drove on to the city of Ulm, where they dropped off von

---

[a] According to Lang's account, they parted in Strasbourg. However, careful analysis of his interview shows that he left them after the Strasbourg incident with the escort. Research and logical study of the map showed that their two paths were identical until Stuttgart, where the road to Lang's town of Schwäbisch-Gemünd continued on east and Rommel's route veered to the southeast. Either Lang or Ryan more than likely noted the wrong town, understandable since they both begin with the same letter.

Tempelhoff and the second driver at the train station. From there, the two took a train to von Tempelhoff's hometown of Munich. Daniel turned the Horch around and drove back Rommel's townhouse in Herrlingen.[148]

---

Corporal Daniel pulled into the home's driveway at 13 Wippengerstrasse[149] around 7 p.m. that evening. The stiff-jointed field marshal got out of the car and stretched. Lucie met her husband at the door, and asked his aide in residence, Captain Hermann Aldinger, to help Daniel bring the bags in, while Rommel went upstairs and changed. Elbo, their dachshund, as always was excited when he spotted the field marshal, and began barking excitedly and jumping up and down, his tail wagging eagerly.[150]

Lucie of course was glad to see him too. She worried so about him, especially when he was running around from one hotspot to the next. He often thought himself charmed, but she knew that one day his luck might turn on him. And on top of that, he looked very tired. The tension was lurking just under his surface. Well, she had made his favorite dish for him—Swabian *Spaetzle mit Kalbsbraten*.[a] That would help.

His son joined them. Manfred, who had recently joined a *Luftwaffe* anti-aircraft defense unit to defend the Swabian capital of Stuttgart against enemy air raids, was granted special leave to see his father and help celebrate his mother's birthday.[151]

At 6'1", the fifteen-year-old now towered over his father. His glasses went well with his quiet demeanor and his dark hair. And when he spoke, it was with a Swabian accent even thicker than his father's.

---

[a] Roast veal stew with German noodles.

They relaxed for a bit as he unwound from the trip. He told them details about the upcoming visit with the Führer, and she worried for him. He did not have the number of men that he needed, and the big panzers were not under his control. Supplies were short, and the Allies were knocking his bridges out. Lucie sympathized.

Later, they sat down to dinner. Rommel commented favorably on the casserole. Since neither he nor Lucie had a taste for wine, they had some blackberry and cherry fruit juices to go with the meal.[152]

After they had eaten and cleaned up the dining room, they sat down again and relaxed. Manfred went to his room to read, while the field marshal talked a bit with his wife.

Since Lucie was going with him to Berchtesgaden, they again talked about their upcoming trip at length. Lucie could see that he seemed depressed about the upcoming meeting with Hitler, and Lucie saw the concern in his eyes. He confided in her about his hopes and expectations of the visit. With Manfred up in his room, Rommel opened himself up to his wife and expressed his most sincere thoughts. As a matter of habit, he had always told her about his current military problems, and somehow she had always understood and made an excellent sounding board for him.[153]

She asked him about the supply problems, and he elaborated. He told her about how cement was hard to get, and about the many different and often obsolete caliber of shells that he had to deal with. He relayed how hard it was getting reinforcements, and about the quality of the recent replacements. He told her about his problems with von Rundstedt, and she nodded sympathetically. He looked at her and told her he desperately hoped the enemy did not invade before he could put more mines down and set up more obstacles. They were just getting into the swing of it. Another month or so…

Lastly, they talked about Hitler himself. They had worried for many months now about his degenerating command capabilities. Rommel told his wife his fear that, if the invasion failed, Hitler would never surrender and take the country down in ruins. They both agreed that he was seriously impaired.

She asked him if he should even be away at this time. He reassured her. The weather was bad. The Allies never launched an invasion in bad weather. No one did. He did not expect any enemy move against him at this time. And anyway, there would have to be a full moon.

The two of them finally retired at 10 p.m.[154] Exhausted from the trip, Rommel fell asleep immediately.

II. June 4th—The Trip Home					Rommel's Fateful Trip Home

# III. June 5th

## "The Old Man's gone away."

*9:30 p.m., British Double Summer Time.* Eisenhower, dressed as always in his olive green battle dress uniform, walked into the library of his headquarters at Southwick Manor. The time had come for him and all of his senior staff members to decide as to whether to give the word to start Operation Neptune, or to delay the invasion again to at least mid-late June, or maybe even mid-July.[155]

British Chief Meteorologist Stagg started the meeting off by reporting that if the invasion had taken place on the 5th as originally planned, with the weather being as bad as it was, the operation would have been a total catastrophe. He then delivered the good news that electrified the tension in the room. An upcoming three-day period of barely tolerable conditions was still scheduled to arrive early in the morning, and at the moment appeared to not only be on track, but also include better conditions than first estimated. The rain would subside substantially, and the 25-30 knot winds would abate some. Cloud coverage would still be heavy, but not continuous. And by Tuesday morning, visibility would be good enough to allow close naval fire support to spot their assigned targets.[156]

Eisenhower was faced with a tremendous decision. Another postponement could easily spell disaster. The next tolerable tidal period would start on June 19th; but it would be moonless. To wait until July would add enormous security risks in keeping the time and place of the invasion secret, not to mention giving the enemy more precious time to prepare.

On the other hand, there was no promise that this short break in the weather would last. To make matters worse, postponing the invasion by 24 hours has meant that, should he decide to give the word to go on the 6th, low tide would occur about an hour later, coming now at 5:15.[a] The U.S. landings would therefore be at least an hour later, coming between 06:15 and 06:45 BDST.[157]

Eisenhower turned to each of his commanders one by one for their opinions. His chief of staff, Bedell Smith, thought they should do it. The air commanders, Air Chief Marshals Tedder and Leigh-Mallory were not so sure. Montgomery, like yesterday, wanted to go. They discussed it some more.[158]

At 9:45 p.m., Eisenhower made his decision. The invasion would go forward.[159]

The orders went out at once to the Allied fleets. Over 6,000 ships[b] of all types began to set sail once again from various points in England.[160] Spearheading the task forces were waves of various-sized fleet and coastal minesweepers.[161] They would have to clear wide channels through the German minefields so that the task forces could safely pass through.

The 1200-plus warships in these fleets included six battleships.[c] Among them was the old USS Nevada, crusty

---

[a] Many sources have indicated that the Allies (specifically, the Americans) hit the beaches exactly at low tide. This was not the case, especially since the invasion was postponed a day. The first waves of Americans came ashore at or near 0630 hours, BDST. Extrapolating data taken from the *English Channel Handbook* prepared by the British Admiralty and included with U.S. all Navy operational orders, low tide on Utah Beach would be about 0512, and about 05:18 for Omaha Beach, BDST. Low tide at the British beaches would occur around 0526.

[b] Exact figures of course vary. Many sources claim the Allied fleets totaled about 5,000 vessels, but they usually do not include smaller craft or landing craft carried aboard transports. Other sources put the number closer to 7,000.

[c] *USS Arkansas, USS Texas, USS Nevada, HMS Warspite, HMS Ramilles*. The sixth, *HMS Rodney* (the focus of the Eastern Task Force Reserve), was present off Sword Beach on the 6th, but returned to the Spithead naval assembly area the same day, and did not start actively participating *(Cont.)*

*veteran of Pearl Harbor. Steaming beside them were dozens of smaller destroyers and destroyer escorts, a couple dozen cruisers, and a thousand smaller escort craft.* [162] *The assault flotilla, the vital key to the entire operation consisted of over 4,000 amphibious assault vessels and included some 1,500 landing craft.* [163]

*At 4:15 a.m. (BDST), Eisenhower met one more time with his staff, reassessed the weather forecast, and after some deliberation, he ordered the "It's on" messages be sent to confirm the invasion date for the 6th.*

*There was now no turning back.* [164]

---

Throughout June 5th, nothing unusual was reported to *Heeresgruppe B*. There had been no recon flights this month, so no photo-intelligence reports had to be analyzed. There was in short, nothing that plausibly indicated that an invasion might be on its way. On the contrary, it was dreary outside. It rained at times, and the weather stayed bad.

That was all right, though. The field marshal was relaxing at home, so his staff continued their normal, stress-free routine. Admiral Friedrich Ruge, their naval advisor, drove off to Naval Group West to, as he put it, "prod them about the mines."[165]

General Speidel stayed at the château today. He had some personal things to do.

As a matter of fact, he was taking the liberty of inviting by phone a number of guests over for dinner. This included a large number of co-conspirators from the Paris section of the secret anti-Hitler resistance. With unusual Teutonic humor,

---

in covering the landings until June 7th. A seventh battleship, *Rodney's* sister ship *HMS Nelson*, came across the Channel and joined the fleet four days later.

he prefaced his unexpected invitations with the wry phrase: "The Old Man's gone away"[166].

Speidel's dinner was going to have a number of interesting guests. Among them was to be his brother-in-law Dr. Max Horst, who worked in military administration for the Military Governor of France. There was of course the outspoken author and philosopher Ernst Jünger,[a] now a captain serving in that command, and 'war reporter' Major Wilhelm von Schramm, who was a good friend of his.[167]

Most all of these guests were members of the central France cell of the resistance movement, committed to overthrowing Hitler. Jünger was bringing with him a secret, 20-page document[168] that he had written. It described a detailed plan on how they intended to make peace with the Allies after the Führer was either overthrown and imprisoned, or just killed. Speidel eagerly looked forward to the evening. He told his friend von Schramm when he phoned him, "We can really have a night discussing things."[169]

---

Rommel was enjoying the day at home, lounging around in relaxed civilian attire with Lucie and Manfred.[170] With them was Mrs. Hildegarde Kirchheim,[b] whose husband had

---

[a] Jünger had for years opposed Hitler's regime. Still, he was mostly allowed to voice his opinion (one of the few authors left in the Reich that could do so) because of his reputation as an accomplished author, and his strong ties to the military. He was also a decorated veteran of World War I, having been awarded Germany's highest honor, the *Pour le Mérite* ("Blue Max"), one of the youngest soldiers to ever receive the award.

[b] Her husband, *Generalleutnant* Heinrich Kirchheim, was originally with the War Office as an authority on tropical warfare. He later transferred to North Africa in February of 1941, and then to Rommel's staff in late April of 1941. Rommel, chose him to replace Colonel Johannes Streich to command the Fifth Light Division, at the time was in the middle of an
*(Cont.)*

been with Rommel early-on in North Africa, and Rommel's sister Helene had dropped in as well. Aldinger took some photos of them all to mark the occasion.

Early that morning, he went to his study, so that he could start writing a report to the Führer about why the disposition of the panzers should be changed. He would state that he needed five panzer divisions and that at least one of those now a part of OKW Reserves should be placed at the base of the Carentan Peninsula. Probably the 12th SS Panzer.[171]

During the day, von Tempelhoff telephone Rommel at his home. Rommel told him that no appointment with the Führer had been set yet, but that he expected to get a confirming appointment very soon. He added, "I'll ring you as soon as I hear, and then I will pick you up and we'll go down to Berchtesgaden together."

Von Tempelhoff acknowledged and as they said their good-byes, he added, "Say hello to your wife."[172]

Rommel checked in by phone with General Schmundt, Hitler's adjutant, to arrange for a meeting with the Führer. Examining their schedule, Schmundt replied that the Führer would probably have some time to see him in the next day or two—probably on Thursday, the 8th. Schmundt would call him back later to confirm this.[a][173]

In the meantime, he was thoroughly luxuriating in his time at home, relieved of the tensions of command. He had several conversations with his wife and their guests, and Manfred sat in on some of them. He told them about the heavy enemy air activity, and the constant bombing of the

---

assault against the heavy Tobruk fortifications. When Kirchheim's attack failed to take the strategic port, Rommel made a thorough job of chewing him out—an insult the general never forgot. Kirchheim was now serving in the Replacement Army High Command.

[a] When the invasion came, Schmundt would be the only member of the German high command that would know that Rommel is in Germany.

railroads. When asked what could be done to improve the situation, he thought about it.

"You know, we should use the French canals and rivers to move up our supplies and reinforcements…"

Manfred asked how.

"Well, we could use specially-built concrete boats, which could be easily camouflaged, and they would move at night. This would give us an extra arm in our supply problem."

That evening, he had another nice dinner with his family, and afterwards, they discussed the idea of glass mines.

Everyone went to bed early. [174]

---

*The Allied fleet stayed undetected throughout the day, mostly because the large convoys were just beginning to sail, and because the Germans felt that the seas were still too rough to send their outpost ships[175] or patrolling E-boats out. If they were to come out now and spot the invasion fleet, they would be able to give the defenders a precious 10-14 hours of advanced warning. It would also give Rommel time enough to get back to La Roche-Guyon before midnight.*

*Meanwhile, thousands of Resistance fighters, alerted by certain prepared, coded messages broadcast that evening by the BBC, were getting ready to execute dozens of different sabotage missions against their oppressors. They carefully uncovered hidden explosives, detonators, guns, knives, and other weapons or equipment that they would need to use in the next 48 hours for their individual assignments.*

*Each of their missions had some significance to the upcoming invasion, and all of them were designed to disrupt communications, destroy or delay supplies, and in general further isolate the western part of France.[176]*

At La Roche-Guyon, Hans Speidel and his invited guests were spending an interesting evening in the château. There were a number of discussions about a variety of subjects, both before and during the sumptuous dinner. They chatted about the situation in Italy and of course, the recent setbacks in Russia. A couple French subjects came up, including French literature, politics and their navy. Conditions in the United States were discussed, initially directed, no doubt, at Consul-General Pfeiffer's presence; he had just come from there. Closer to the main theme of the evening, they also talked about "the insufficient development of Hitler's future plans."[177]

After dinner and despite the weather, several guests took a number of brief walks around the beautiful villa, gazing out that evening over the lovely Seine valley, commenting on the unusual air activity in the bad weather. Eventually, most of the guests split up into two groups.

One bunch sat around in one of the parlors sipping brandy and cognac, while a colonel told a number of amusing stories. The second group, the plotters, went into a small anteroom just off the main dining salon. There, sipping coffee, they went over Jünger's 30-page written peace proposal, entitled *Der Friede.*[a] To be shown to the Allies after Hitler's demise, it gave a detailed plan on how the conspirators would make peace with the Allies after the Führer is removed, and plans to create a new united Europe. Methods to involve the field marshal in their group were also discussed. They after all needed his name to give credence to their coup, if and when it occurred.[178]

They had been steadily working on how they could win him over for weeks now. It would not be an easy task.

---

[a] "The Peace." Jünger had started the document in 1943, but it would not be published in its entirety until 1947.

### III. June 5th

Rommel had been a staunch supporter of the Führer. Even though he was disillusioned over the war, he would not be easily inclined to go against his mentor and be involved in a coup. The plotters decided to let Speidel continue approaching him. Speidel knew that he had to proceed cautiously. On the other hand, he had established a good rapport with his superior, and so their talk could be informal.

Just after 10 p.m., Speidel received a call from the army group's Intelligence Chief, Colonel Anton Staubwasser, who was downstairs at the operations desk. When Speidel picked up the receiver, Staubwasser told him in a somewhat worried tone that the second part of the Verlaine poem had been intercepted.[179]

Speidel had no idea what that meant. He told Staubwasser so.

The Intelligence Officer patiently reminded him of the Verlaine warning messages. He explained that, according to Meyer at Fifteenth Army Intelligence, the Verlaine poem was considered a key link to the invasion date, based upon reliable information that had come in a few months ago from the now-defunct *Abwehr*. When the second verse was transmitted, the invasion would supposedly come in the next couple of days. That, Meyer had concluded, would make the target date tomorrow the sixth, or the next day, the seventh. Staubwasser also added that General von Salmuth had, as a result, put the Fifteenth Army on the alert. Perhaps, he suggested, General Dollmann should do the same with the Seventh.

Speidel replied he would come over to talk about it and hung up the phone.

Politely excusing himself from his guests, he calmly left the dinner party and walked down to Operations, where the *Ic* was working. They discussed the problem face to face. Speidel finally told Staubwasser to call *OB West* and ask them whether or not the Seventh Army should be alerted. "Go with what they say," said Speidel. He then casually returned to his dinner party.[180]

Staubwasser made the call to *OB West*, and an arrogant senior staff member there told him that Seventh Army need not be alerted. So the army defending Normandy was not given such an order.[181]

---

*11 p.m. It was a dark night, with only occasional glimpses of the moon from the ground through a low cloud blanket.[182] Cloud cover was about 5/10ths, cloud height was low at about 600 feet.[183]*

*Several dozen Allied aircraft were roaming over this part of the northern French countryside. Northeast of Caen, six gliders carried pathfinders of the British 6th Airborne Division are quietly sailing down towards the Orne River/Caen Canal bridges to seal off the British bridgehead's left flank from mobile counterattack. They would shortly be followed by more pathfinders to prepare three drop zones east of the Orne Canal for the unit's two parachute brigades.[184]*

*Roughly 50 miles to the west, American Dakotas carrying pathfinders of the U.S. 82nd and 101st Airborne Divisions began their final approach into pre-specified zones over the Cotentin peninsula of Normandy. Their mission was to prepare and light the drop zones within a dark, 50-square mile area for the bulk of the two airborne divisions which would begin coming down in a little over an hour.[185]*

*At other various points all over Normandy, a number of other transports started dumping half-size, lifelike paratroop dummies, equipped with pintail bombs, mini-flares, and firecrackers. As these dummies came down and landed all over the Norman countryside, their fireworks displays begin to flash all over the cloudy sky, simulating rifle and light machine-gun fire from German forces below.[186]*

III. June 5th                                   Rommel's Fateful Trip Home

*Erwin Rommel, Befehlshaber, Heeresgruppe B*

*Generalfeldmarschall Gerd von Rundstedt, OB West, Rommel's superior*

*Rommel inspecting the defenses of the Atlantic Wall in April, 1944, 1944.*

*Vizeadmiral Friedrich Ruge, Rommel's chief Naval advisor.*

*Generalleutnant Dr. Hans Speidel, Chief of Staff, Heeresgruppe B, 1944.*

*Rommel and his driver, Karl Daniel, in France, 1944.*

III. June 5th                               Rommel's Fateful Trip Home

*General Sinnhuber, General Speidel, Rommel's aide Captain Helmuth Lang, and Rommel, April 18, 1944*

*Manfred, Rommel, and Lucie-Marie, taken around 1941. Some three years later, the son would be taller than his father.*

*All photos courtesy of the U.S. National Archives or Bundsarchives in Germany.*

# IV. June 6th—Morning

"Well, find out—and FAST."

Hans Speidel was tired. He had been up most of the night. And the spirits from the party he had thrown together the night before had not helped his head. Now, though he really needed sleep, he was up to his neck in operational problems. Some lines of communication were out, making things worse.

Despite what the weather forecasts had predicted, alarming messages had been coming in to *Heeresgruppe B* all through the night. Some sort of major airborne drop had come down along the Orne River on the right, around Caen, and another had landed over on the left, near the Vire and Merderet Rivers, and around Ste-Mère-Église. Chances are, any landing would be somewhere in the middle, although that was in no way certain, since they were getting reports of enemy airborne activity from Calais to Cherbourg. And along the Straits of Dover, there were a couple reports of engine noises over the water. An invasion fleet?

There was one message that paratrooper straw-and-rubber dummies had been dropped just west of General Marcks' LXXXIV Corps headquarters in St. Lô. There were also many messages of multi-engine aircraft (probably heavy bombers) passing overhead, from the Channel Islands, west of the Cherbourg peninsula, to the Somme Estuary. There were several reports, especially one from the Channel Islands, specifying that the aircraft were flying slowly—probably towing gliders.[187]

Speidel cleared his mind. He had to separate the confusing and misleading from the accurate, if he was to get any kind of reliable picture as to what was going on, and what these air drops meant. Certainly this was nothing to wake Field Marshal Rommel about—at least not yet. Speidel did not by any means have a good idea of what was developing, and he did not want to look scatter-brained to the Old Man. Besides, so far they had things well in hand. A phone call some time tomorrow to his home would be appropriate, just to fill him in on the airborne landings.

Right now though, the situation was vague. He did not know if there was going to be a landing or not; but if there was, he certainly did not want to commit what reserves he controlled to the wrong area. Of course, he could do that deliberately. IF the Allies landed elsewhere, and IF they succeeded in getting a foothold on the continent, and IF the field marshal was right about not being able to dislodge them once they were firmly ashore, then the war would by all means definitely be lost. That madman in Berlin would then have no choice but to step down as their leader.

In the meantime, Speidel had to consider that Rommel might be correct. Defeating the invasion seemed like the only way to provide them with a negotiating tool against the Allies. So where and when he committed the reserve panzers was crucial. Not wanting to err, he decided not to commit them at all. At least not yet.

It was almost 4 a.m.[188]

---

*By 3:40 a.m., assault craft were being lowered from Allied transports in preparation for the landings that would soon follow. Hundreds of Allied soldiers soon began to warily descend swaying nets into scores of landing craft. A half hour later, as Allied aircraft roared overhead, the first wave of American assault craft began their dark 1-1/2 hour trip in towards the beaches. They had an 11-1/2 mile run along five sea lanes marked with buoys for traffic control.*[189]

*The Normandy landing had begun.*

*Some thirty minutes after the soldiers climbed into the landing craft, the Allied warships began their massive bombardment of the coast.*[190] *Scores of projectiles of all calibers started slamming into the beaches from many different distances and angles. In addition, swarms of Allied bombers flew inland over the clouds, headed for coastal targets, and unworried about any interdiction from the Luftwaffe.*[191]

*Meanwhile, inland and far away from the shelling, the three panzer divisions closest to the Normandy area were all biding their time, still in or near the same areas that they had occupied since midnight. The 12th SS Panzer Division was taking some initiative and scouting out the local areas, with one regiment reconnoitering up the road towards Caen and another out looking for paratroopers that had been reported*[192] *nearby.*[a] *The massive Panzer Lehr Division was spread out all around near the town of Chartres, the men standing around talking and smoking, ready to move.*[193]

*The 21st Panzer was the closest armored division to the invasion area. Many of its units had been given marching orders and were technically on the move, although they were not really making much headway. Most of the division was experiencing traffic problems approaching Caen from the south. One panzergrenadier regiment, positioned to the right of the city, had sent forward a few patrols and was poised to attack reported paratrooper landings along the eastern bank of the Orne River. They were expecting the go-ahead to start a major advance to recapture the two bridges across the river and the parallel canal. All requests by the units to advance resulted in the same answer—get in position on the road, be ready to move out, and hold until further orders.*[194]

---

[a] The report was false.

## IV. June 6th—Morning  Rommel's Fateful Trip Home

It was quiet at the Rommel home in Herrlingen. Dawn was nearing. A few birds chirped in the distance; otherwise, it was the peaceful silence of another day in a beautiful small town.

By the time the field marshal was up, there were a number of people in or near the villa besides him and his wife Lucie. There was of course Manfred, and the servants, Karolina and Private Loitsl. There was also their houseguest Mrs. Kirchheim, and Daniel, his driver. Manfred who had recently joined a *Luftwaffe* anti-aircraft defense unit to defend the Swabian capital of Stuttgart against enemy air raid was there on special leave to see his father and help celebrate his mother's birthday.

---

*At 0630 hours BDST, there was on the Normandy beaches a light mist that combined with dust and the acrid smells of cordite smoke in the air, created by the explosions from the guns of the naval bombardment.*[195] *U.S. troops began to land among the obstacles at the water's edge along two stretches of Calvados shore that they have designated Utah and Omaha beaches. It was H-Hour for the Americans.*

*Along Utah's nine-mile beach, as a number of scattered German strongpoints tensely awaited them,*[196] *many American landing craft approached and then slammed into the beach. The ramps crashed down, and the American troops scrambled ashore with little opposition.*[197]

*At Omaha beach to the east though, it was quite a different story. The worst fears of the assaulting troops were about to be realized. The battle-hardened 916th Infantry and the well-defended 726th Grenadier Regiments were waiting for the landing craft to come into range. Their well-concealed main batteries were mostly still intact, partly because the Allied aircraft, to make sure they hit land and not water's edge, had delayed toggling their bombs for several seconds, and had thus missed most of the batteries overlooking the beaches.*

*The German defenders held off their small arms fire until the assault craft were about a quarter-mile away. They then opened up with a terrific tumult, pouring a devastating fusillade into the boats struggling to make it to the beach with their loads.*

*Some craft, damaged or desperate to drop their men before they were hit, lowered their ramps early. The GIs not immediately hit by fire jumped into the surf, only to find themselves in a desperate struggle to keep from drowning as they sank down to the channel floor under their heavy loads. The surviving craft reached the water's edge and lowered their bow ramps into the surf, exposing the men inside to the murderous machine-gun fire coming from the bluffs above. The GIs stumbled forward into the deep swirling waters, and many of them were mowed down like wheat. Those that somehow survived the heavy fire and made it into the surf alive under heavy fire desperately tried with their heavy loads of weapons and ammo to stay afloat and wade through the water, stumble shore, and lumber across the beaches, out in the open, and in clear view to the enemy shooting down at them.*

*Death awaited the Americans.*[198]

*Although the British and Canadians were scheduled to hit Gold, Juno, and Sword beaches between 0600 and 0630,*[199] *they decided to go in later than the Americans, and thereby catch the tide coming back in. This would help them avoid many of the relatively few low tide obstacles, while giving the warships more time to bombard the shore.*[200] *Unfortunately, the seas were determined to be too rough for any more delays, so the British and Canadians began heading towards the beaches. They immediately ran into problems making headway in the choppy waters.*

## IV. June 6th—Morning      Rommel's Fateful Trip Home

*The British finally began hitting Gold Beach about 0630, and Sword Beach some five minutes later. The Canadians began landing at Juno beach from 0645 to 0655.*[201]

---

Staff members at Rommel's headquarters were optimistic about the whole idea of a possible landing. Many of the personnel, up most of the night, turned in or went back to bed.[202]

*OB West* had ordered the reserve panzer divisions towards the coast. No one knew that Jodl and OKW had countermanded the order.

The 21st Panzer Division, alerted since midnight, was by this time moving towards their organizational areas, still awaiting the official word from Rommel's headquarters to advance.[203] So in addition to the units mobilized and ready on the coast, they assumed that three full panzer divisions were either on their way or prepared to strike into the troubled area. And all the divisions in the army group were on full alert. German forces everywhere in Normandy were already reacting to the reports of airborne landings. And wherever else the Allies struck, from Calais to St. Malo, they would be smashed and driven back into the sea.[204]

Unfortunately, no one thought to remember General Pickert and the bulk of his III Flak Corps, with three of its four flak regiments out of the landing area, stationed all around the Somme River. The flak units would not start for Normandy until late that afternoon.[205]

---

Rommel was up at the crack of dawn, enjoying a leisurely morning at his home. Usually, he would get up a bit later and go for a walk—still back in time, of course, to listen to the news on their radio at 7 a.m. Then it would be a brisk bath, a shave, getting dressed, and then a clear soup breakfast, cooked for him by his wife, Lucie.[206]

However, today was different. This was a special day. This was Lucie's 50th birthday. So he was up very early. On her behalf, he had arranged with the servants to have bouquets of sweet-smelling flowers from the fields in each room of the villa. And the night before, he had carefully gathered his wife's presents into the drawing room and had put them on the table in there. Later that morning, he would lay them out and prepare them nicely, putting last minute touches here and there. He was assisted in this task by his wife's guest, Mrs. Kirchheim.

Naturally, the handmade Parisian shoes that he had bought for Lucie were to be the centerpiece of the gift array.[207] A special edition,[208] they were platform-style pumps, with black heels. The upper portions were made of soft gray suede, and as a layer in the sole, there was a suede strip that ran around the shoe. And of course, they were her size: 5-1/2.[209]

He smiled in anticipation of how she would react when she saw them. This would indeed be a good day. In the meantime, he was going to have a nice, leisurely morning, relax, and perhaps later, review his upcoming meeting with the Führer.

At around 5 o'clock that morning,[210] the telephone rang.[a] Surprised, Rommel, still wearing his dressing gown,

---

[a] Many sources, including General Speidel himself, state that he made the first or the only phone call (depending on the source) between 6 and 6:30 a.m., presumably *British Double Summer Time* (BDST); but the headquarters war diary logged only one call to Rommel, and that was at 10:15 German Central Time (GCT). (Mitcham, p.76, from Ryan, p.284, and CRC-26/5-WD, p.7)

Regarding the time and number of phone calls, two of Ryan's sources seem the most reliable. One was an interview with Manfred Rommel on July 9, 1958 (CRC-27/8), some 14 years later, and another one was with Lang at his home in Gemünd the same day (CRC-26/25). Each states that *(Cont.)*

## IV. June 6th—Morning    Rommel's Fateful Trip Home

the first phone call came around 5 a.m. (certainly early enough in the morning), and that the second call came later at the verified time of 10:15. Also, Speidel told Ryan in an interview that he called Rommel initially 'around 6 a.m.," but Ryan dismissed the call in his book (Ryan, p.284), despite corroborative testimony given by Lang and Manfred Rommel of an earlier call. Koch (CRC-27/8-Koch, p. 5) states in his book (*Erwin Rommel, die Wandlung eines grossen Soldaten*) that Lucie-Marie told him the first call came around 6:30 a.m.

This second 10:15 a.m. call is given credence by the fact that General Speidel was not notified of any actual landings until General Pemsel (Seventh Army chief of staff at Le Mans) called him around 9:05 a.m. (Pemsel did call at 6:15 a.m. to report a naval bombardment, but Speidel concluded that its purpose was not clear, and that it might be a diversion for an attack elsewhere). Testimony from Mrs. Kirchheim, who happened to be at the Rommel home in Herrlingen that day, also supports the 10:15 call time (See Irving, p. 442), as does of course, the army group war diary, and the second call was in German Central Time (GCT), verified as such by the Army Group B Telephone Log.

Testimonies given by Lang and Tempelhoff are enough evidence to support Speidel's claim that there were indeed at least two phone calls. Perhaps General Speidel's time of 6 a.m. was just an estimate,. This discrepancy would then confirm both Capt. Lang's and Manfred Rommel's claims of the first call at 5 a.m. (CRC-26/25.8, CRC-27/8.4). I am here assuming that this time is correct for the purposes of this narrative. [*Auth.*]

On the other hand, David Fraser (*Knight's Cross*) wrote that Speidel first called Rommel at 06:30 a.m. to tell him about the airdrops, but that Rommel later called HIM back at 10:00 a.m. It was at that time, Fraser wrote, that the field marshal was first told by Speidel about the amphibious landings that had occurred on the Normandy coast (Fraser, p. 485).

Unfortunately for the modern historian, a number of omissions and 'corrections' were later made to the army group War Diary. General Speidel admitted this after the war. Instructions for these changes came from or were made by Rommel, Speidel himself, or by the Operations Officer, Col. von Tempelhoff (Irving, p.433). Ostensibly, the 'adjustments' were made to prevent any sort of retribution upon anyone concerned when Adolf Hitler himself ordered a subsequent investigation. Suspicious and smelling treason in the air, he demanded a full inquiry to find out why so many of the key commanders had been away from their headquarters on the day of the invasion. The log changes in the army group diary were later
*(Cont.)*

went over to the phone to answer it himself.[211] It was his chief of staff at headquarters.

Rommel greeted the Chief amiably, "Well, Speidel. What's up?"[212]

His good mood instantly vanished and he felt himself go numb as Speidel reported that 'some sort of an attack' had been made by the enemy in the night. There had been a number of airborne drops mainly centered around the Normandy area, but some were reported as far northeast as the other side of the Somme River. Details at this point were confusing, and occasionally, one report would seem to contradict another. Speidel concluded that he was not sure whether this was just a limited 'Dieppe-type' of attack—possibly to divert their attention—or the actual invasion.

Rommel replied tersely, "Well, find out—and FAST."[213]

Speidel, unaffected by the sharp retort, acknowledged the order and reported to him what steps he had taken so far. He told Rommel of the countermeasures that had been initiated. The field marshal approved, and added, "I'm returning as fast as I can make it."

Speidel had thought about this. He believed that Rommel should hold off his return, in light of the importance of his trip home, both personal and official (the upcoming meeting with Hitler). Rather, he suggested, the field marshal should wait until he, Speidel could get some more

---

made to protect those individuals who had indeed been away at that time. At Army Group B, they included von Tempelhoff, Captain Lang, and of course, Rommel himself.

A few other sources claim that Rommel received the only word of the invasion between 6 and 7 a.m. (Patrick, p.82) One even wrote that Rommel was in contact with elements of the 1st SS Panzer Corps at 6:30 a.m.(Patrick, p.82). This is highly unlikely. If he was fully alerted before 7 a.m., he certainly would have been dragging his heels in leaving for the front, not having left until about 11:40 a.m. The testimonies of those present at his villa in Herrlingen indicate that he was indeed called early, but not actually informed of the invasion until later in the morning.

IV. June 6th—Morning                    Rommel's Fateful Trip Home

information and better determine exactly what was going on, and as to whether this was an actual invasion or just a diversion. After all, there were no actual sighting reports in as yet of any enemy naval task forces.[a]

Speidel conveyed this to Rommel.[214] "I do not think you should leave right away, *Herr Feldmarschall*," he advised. "But I think that you should wait before making any decision until I ring you back."[b]

Rommel was persuaded by Speidel's logic and (grudgingly) agreed to accept the advice. He hung up the phone and, his mind racing, slowly climbed the stairs to his bedroom. Just in case, he was going to get his things out and start to pack.[215]

---

It was a little after 5 a.m.[c] when Captain Lang's telephone rang in Gemünd. He picked it up and was surprised to hear the field marshal on the other end.

"Lang," he began tensely, "I understand that the invasion has begun; but I'm not sure if this is a Dieppe-type

---

[a] Interestingly though, around 2:30 a.m., Speidel had received a phone call from Max Pemsel at Seventh Army HQ. Pemsel relayed more incoming reports of enemy airborne landings, and one from the Navy that ship engine noises in the Channel had distinctly been heard off the east coast of the Cotentin peninsula. (Patrick, p.81, Brown, p. 65, and CRC-26/6.2) However, this report had not been confirmed by radar, so Speidel dismissed the information, probably assuming that in the most unlikely event the report was true, the noises were most certainly coming from a small number of patrol craft or fishing vessels.

[b] Some theorists later theorized that this also was a deliberate delay by Speidel to keep the field marshal away from the front, but there is no real evidence of that.

[c] Lang gives this time in his interview with Cornelius Ryan. (CRC-26/25-Lang-8)

of raid, or the real thing. So, stand by for further orders—we may be leaving soon."

"*Yawohl, Herr Feldmarschall*," Lang replied in shock.

Rommel hung up and as Lang put down his receiver, as if in a daze, he considered the call. He knew that the field marshal had not yet seen the Führer, so if this was the invasion... Well, Lang fervently hoped that, if this was the real thing, the field marshal could come up with some sort of solution. He always had managed to in the past.

Lang began gathering his clothes and packing them.[216]

---

It was well after 6 a.m. Hans-Georg von Tempelhoff and his wife Maryanne were still asleep, as were the two children, Elizabeth and Howell.

Suddenly, the phone rang, waking him up. He got up in his pajamas to answer it, and as he started downstairs, he noted by the pattern of the rings that this was not a local call. He had learned that local calls were evidenced by a series of weak rings, close together. These tones pulsed much slower and stronger, typical for long distance calls. No, this was a call from outside Munich.[217]

Von Tempelhoff reached the bottom of the stairwell, walked around to the phone, and answered it. The call was from General Speidel at La Roche-Guyon.

"Hello, von Tempelhoff," the chief of staff said calmly. "How are you?"

"I'm quite well," the operations officer replied, puzzled at why the chief of staff was calling this early in the morning just to see how he was.

"My dear Tempelhoff," Speidel said, "I think it'd be a good idea if you came back as soon as possible, because we think it has started."[218]

Von Tempelhoff was stunned. "What has?" he barked. Speidel told him it was the long-awaited invasion.

"Where?!?" he asked, breathless. This just couldn't be happening now.

"Well, yes," Speidel replied. "It looks like north of Caen... in the Cotentin, and from the other side of the Seine, near Le Havre."

It sounded like the entire Normandy area was under assault.

"We're not quite clear. They have some reports of both areas, but I don't think there is any doubt about it."

Rommel had to be told immediately. "What about the field marshal?" von Tempelhoff asked.

"Oh, I've spoken with him, and I think he's already on his way." Speidel reassured him.[a]

Von Tempelhoff had to get back too. Speidel must have asked him if he could leave soon, because he suddenly realized that he was stranded.[219]

"Yes," von Tempelhoff replied, "but right now I have no car. It's down in a workshop, and I think it may take me 10 or noon before I can start!"

Speidel, unperturbed, asked, "Do you remember how you got hold of your driver? What was your driver's name?"

The operations officer told him. His name was Marasch.

"All right," Speidel replied. He told him to call his driver and return as soon as he could.[220]

Hanging up, von Tempelhoff looked over at his Maryanne, who had come down the stairs in her robe. She looked at him and asked, "What's wrong, Hans?"

He told her, and she replied, "I thought so. I thought that must be Speidel."

---

[a] Considering that Speidel had earlier suggested to Rommel that he wait for Speidel's confirmation, Speidel's comment here (if Col. Tempelhoff is correct) must have been to keep the operations officer from worrying. Or else, knowing the field marshal's impatience, Speidel might have taken him at his word that he would be returning immediately, and was conveying that feeling to von Tempelhoff.

Von Tempelhoff went upstairs, washed, shaved, and got dressed. His wife made him breakfast as he called Marasch who lived around Augburg, some 67 km away. His wife answered, and told him that her husband was around the corner in the auto repair shop. Their vehicle was getting serviced, including an oil change.

Von Tempelhoff told her to have Marasch call as soon as he returned.[221]

---

Field Marshal Rommel was up in his bedroom, tensely packing his clothes. Lucie watched him for a bit, and did not say a word. Finally, in a worried tone, he looked over at her and told her that Speidel had reported trouble, and that he might have to return back to France. She let it go at that, but could see that the call had quite upset him.[222]

When he had finished packing, Rommel returned downstairs. Manfred asked him what was going on, and he told the boy what Speidel had reported. The teenager could see that the situation was serious, and although he was not quite sure what was going on, he did grasp the importance of a possible airborne landing. Manfred after all had been schooled in warfare by one of the best, his father, and was himself quite intelligent for a lad of only fifteen.

A little after 7 a.m., Rommel impulsively decided that he was not going to wait for Speidel's second phone call, and was going to just leave. He told Corporal Daniel to get the car ready to travel, and then called Lang back. The aide still had the spare car.

"Lang, meet me at 11 o'clock sharp in Freudenstadt." He did not mention anything more about the possible landing, but he knew the aide would understand.[223]

The hours went by so slowly. Trying to kill some time, Rommel fussed some more with the gift arrangements on the table. The more he tried to act normally, the more concerned he became. What was going on in France? What type of airborne operation were the Allies conducting? Was it a prelude to the main invasion? Or was it some kind of diversion? What were its objectives? And again, most importantly, was any kind of amphibious landing going to follow?

He had no appetite for eating, so he talked some with Manfred. He tried to explain what was going on, and the boy listened attentively.

The time stretched on endlessly. 10 a.m. came and passed, and still no call from Speidel. That was either a good sign or a bad one. Maybe he had tried to call and could not get through. Then again, maybe this airborne thing had been an elaborate hoax. All the more reason to get to Hitler and convince the man to release the reserve panzers to him.

Nervous and worried, the field marshal paced the floor in his drawing room. Sometimes, he would sit for a short while in the drawing room.[224] He even tried to sip some tea.

It was probably too late to call Lang. He most likely was already gone. Well, no matter. The aide would wait for him in Freudenstadt until he arrived…

There was a gentle knock on the door. It was the housemaid, Karolina, and he called her in. Entering the room, she exclaimed breathlessly, *"Herr Feldmarschall* Rommel is wanted on the telephone!" He had not even heard it ring. It was 10:15 a.m.[a]

Rommel hurried over to the phone. This was either Speidel with an update, or General Schmundt in Berchtesgaden, wanting to set up a scheduled time for Rommel's meeting with the Führer.

---

[a] All valid sources agree on the time of the second call—10:15 a.m. This is documented by the Army Group B Phone Log (U.S. National Archives, MS. X-511), which also indicated that Speidel initiated the call.

He picked up the receiver and said, "Yes, Rommel here." It was not Schmundt though; it was his chief of staff on the line.

Rommel's curiosity swiftly moved into heavy shock as Speidel informed him that the invasion had begun.

"What?!? What?!?" he half-shouted. "Where?!?"

It was at Normandy. The Chief added some early details—the airborne landings, the naval assault, cut communications... Rommel listened in silence, the blood draining from his face. He just stood there, stunned by what he had heard.[225] The Allies had pulled a big one over on him. And he had just wasted over four hours to find out for sure. He should not have waited for Speidel's call. He should have just departed immediately.

Lucie, having come into the room while he was on the phone, could tell immediately that the call had changed him. Her husband was now terribly upset, and there seemed to be a thick layer of tension in the room.[226]

"I'll return at once!" he finally barked. He quickly added that he would stop in Rheims and call for an update. In the meantime, there defenses were to hold at all costs. The enemy, he instructed, had to be pinned down on the beaches. Then he slammed the receiver down.[227]

He turned to Lucie, staring at him. "The invasion has begun, " he told her tersely." I must return immediately."[228]

He stood there, still bewildered, absorbing Speidel's report. Staring at the wall, he finally commented softly, "How stupid of me... How stupid of me..."[229]

His mind was lost in a jumble of thoughts. Regaining his composure, he yanked the receiver up again. When an operator came on the line, he barked, "A *Führungsblitz*[a] call to the Führer's headquarters, at once!"[230]

---

[a] An emergency command call, taking priority over any other telephone line/call then being placed (Irving, p.442).

The operator hesitated. Such an order had tremendous ramifications for her. It carried absolute top priority in the telephone system. Not just anybody could order such a thing, and the poor girl hesitated, not knowing whether to really clear the line for him or not.

"Dammit, girl," he snapped impatiently, "this is ROMMEL speaking! Give me a line right now!"

That did it. His call finally went through, and he reported to OKW what he knew of the situation, and that he was returning to his headquarters immediately.

When the call was finished, he ran upstairs to change into his uniform. Confronting his male servant, Private Rudolf Loistl, he ordered, "Get my Daniel up here with the car at once." Just in case, they had better make sure Lang had gone. "And get Lang to meet me at Freudenstadt," he added.[231]

Luckily, Lang had not left yet. Loistl got him on the phone, and Rommel spoke briefly to him. He mentioned his intentions to return, and the need for haste. He told the aide to meet him in Freudenstadt at noon now,[232] instead of 11 a.m.[a]

---

Lang slowly hung up the phone, shaken by the second phone call. Clearly, the field marshal was deeply upset. Lang had heard it in his voice during the first phone call. On top of

---

[a] The time conflicts with Lang's interview after the war. Ryan's book actually states a rendezvous time of 1 a.m., though Lang claims he met Rommel in Freudenstadt and they left there at 11 a.m. GCT (CRC-26/25, p.9) That does not make sense, though. From each of their homes to Freudenstadt is about 140 km (87 miles), which is a good hour and a half drive, even at high speeds. So Ryan's 1 p.m. time might be correct, especially if Rommel did not leave immediately (Ryan wrote that Rommel called Lang twice in the next 45 minutes).

that, the field marshal had then changed his plans. And he was *never* indecisive about anything.

Lang snapped out of the daze and began to act. He briefly told his mother what he was doing, then went to his room and began packing feverishly for the return trip. Why the change in time? Probably so that Lang could get there in time. Then what? Return to France, probably. Naturally, there was no time to see the Führer now.[233]

Lang left his mother around 10:30 a.m.,[234] heading for Freudenstadt via Stuttgart.[235]

---

Well obviously, Lucie's birthday party was ruined. Corporal Daniel went outside to bring the car around, while Lucie and Manfred gathered at the door with the field marshal. He said his goodbyes to his family behind the closed front door, as he always did.[a] Worry was clearly evident on his face.

When he heard the car approach, he kissed Lucie and then turned to his teenage son and gently put his hand on his head. "Well, Manfred," he said gently, "you and I will try and win the war."[236]

The boy tried to smile up at his father, and replied, "*Auf Wiedersehen, Papa.*" With that, the field marshal turned and climbed into the front seat of the Horch. He glanced up at his family before Daniel started them down the driveway. It was about 10:40 a.m.[237]

Lucie watched him leave, and then turned to go back inside. A few minutes later, she came into Frau Kircheim's room and in an agitated voice told her guest that Erwin had

---

[a] According to Frau Rommel, the field marshal did not like to physically show any affection towards his family whenever staff members were present.

already left for France.[238] She added that she was worried, both for him, and for Germany itself. The two ladies talked for a while about the phone call.

Finally, resigned to another birthday without her husband and disheartened by his abrupt departure, Lucie picked up and opened his birthday gift.

It was a pair of elegant, stylish, gray Parisian pumps shoes that he had prided himself on getting her. She read the label: D I 5-1/2 L. She slowly tried them on.

They did not even fit her.[239]

# V.- Rommel Heads Back
## "I was right all along..."

Having left his home in Gemünd, Lang, his foot heavy on the accelerator, raced down the highway, heading towards Freudenstadt to meet up with the field marshal. Lang appreciated the time factor and tore through the countryside, stopping only when he absolutely had to. He had boldly driven straight through the city of Stuttgart at a frightening pace, at times going over 95 kph, blasting his horn[240] and at times waving impatiently as he scared the hell out of the many city residents who happened to be out.

Finally around midday, after what seemed like an eternity, he roared into the town of Freudenstadt and parked the car. Rommel arrived shortly thereafter, and together with Daniel at the wheel (Lang was thankful), they started out towards France. The Operations Officer was not with them, since they had not had time to coordinate a rendezvous. No matter. Speidel had reassured Rommel that he had also telephoned Templehoff that morning,[241] so they presumed that he was making his own arrangements to return, either in his own car, or in another government vehicle. It was just as well. Rommel was not going to wait for him.

Daniel silently drove at a good clip, with Rommel sitting as usual in front next to him. In the back, Lang slowly recovered from his headlong race across the southern German countryside. Gazing at the field marshal in front, he could see that the boss was terribly upset.[242] That was understandable, considering that the invasion had started and they were on leave.

By one o'clock, Freudenstadt was well behind them. As the Horch raced across the countryside, the minutes ticked by. Rommel stared glumly at the road ahead.[243]

The field marshal was understandably impatient with their progress, and it contributed to his depression. The critical battle, upon which so much depended, the struggle that his men knew they had to win, had started over thirteen hours ago in his absence. Every minute that he was away was like another drop of blood in the life of Germany falling to the ground. He had to get back soon. Why couldn't his car go faster?

Far up ahead of him at the Calvados beaches, his *Feldgrau* were fighting the most important battle of their lives, and their leader, the great Desert Fox, was taking a joy ride across France. They had consistently, faithfully supported him, and in the past had readily fought and died for him, not just because he was such a knowledgeable, charismatic commander, but because he was always right next to them, usually in the worst sector, sharing their dangers, joking with them, encouraging them, coordinating them, often commanding desperate situations right from their midst. He had learned in the desert back in 1942 that when they talked about following him anywhere, their favorite expression[244] was *Er hat die Strapazen mitgemacht.*[a] Well, he had certainly missed the boat this time. They had been hit hard by the enemy, and he was at home, lounging around. His *Fingerspitzengefuehl* that had worked so well in North Africa had failed him.

It just was not fair. He had sacrificed so much for so many months, and now at the most critical time, he had taken a chance on the weather and had erred in going home. Hitler would be furious of course, and probably not care for his motives or listen to his reasons. He would just scream out at him. And if the enemy could not be thrown back into the sea, the field marshal would permanently lose his stature. He might get sacked, perhaps even arrested.

---

[a] "He shared the gaff;" i.e., he shared the hardship with them.

Worse than all of than that, Germany itself would suffer terribly. It could not hope to win a three-front war against the British, the Americans and the Russians. The German people would end up fighting and dying to the very end as their country was reduced to total ruins. And the Führer would probably let them all be sacrificed for the glory of the Reich. He had once said so.[a]

No, he would probably never surrender. Besides, he could not anyway, even if he wanted to. No Allied country would now negotiate with him. So Germany just had to turn back the invasion, just to hope to survive. In the meantime though, Rommel's men were caught up in that struggle, even now fighting for their lives without him. And the panzers that they so desperately needed were inland...

Abruptly Rommel turned around to face Lang and said pointedly, "You see, Lang? I was right all the time. I should have had the *Panzer Lehr* and the 12th SS under my command near the beaches..."[b] He trailed off, lost in

---

[a] Last July, Hitler had made a cold comment about Germany's fate to Rommel, something that had stunned the field marshal (not the first time he had made such a remark, but the first time Rommel had heard such a comment). Hitler, evaluating their chances of a final victory in the East, had once again taken up a favorite theme of his—the ultimate effort. He was convinced that Germany would still win the war if only the Germans would rise and be the great warriors that he knew they were, and to make the same supreme effort that he himself, their supreme leader, was making every day. As his eyes suddenly blazed, he suddenly had become defiantly bitter. "Well, if the German people are incapable of winning the war," he had said vehemently, "then they can ROT." (Lewin, p.209, Majdalany, p.255, Rommel, p.428, and Marshall, p.235)

Rommel of course had been stunned to hear him say that. Hitler had then added, "In any case, the best of them are already dead. If I'm to be beaten, then I will fight for every single house. Absolutely nothing will be left standing." (Marshal, p.235)

[b] Ryan's account in *The Longest Day* strangely differs from the notes he took. According to the book, Freudenstadt was a good two hours behind them when Rommel made this remark. In the interview with Lang *(Cont.)*

thought, then turned back around and stared silently once again at the road ahead.[245]

The sedan raced along the highway, leaving small dust swirls behind it, and occasionally throwing up a spray of water as it hit a puddle left over by the recent rains. Daniel, usually a careful driver, was ignoring nearly all of the speed limits they came across, only slowing down for heavy traffic, downtown sections, pedestrians (despite the situation, the field marshal did not want them to run over anyone), and occasional road-crossing farm animals. They briefly stopped at the checkpoints, and avoided any low-flying enemy aircraft.

At one point, Rommel, going over in his mind reinforcements for the landing area, thought of all the air force personnel. "If we only had our 30,000 *Luftwaffe*, who are idling in the streets without planes, no landing would have occurred."[246]

Lang, sitting in back alone, finally tried to engage the field marshal in a conversation about the reported landings. His attempt failed. Rommel did not want to talk. He simply stared ahead, silently, sightlessly. Lang did not know how to approach him, or to help. Self-recrimination for a brilliant man could often be merciless…[247]

Rommel suddenly turned around again and grumbled, "Lang, just imagine! The invasion has begun and we didn't even know about it. No reconnaissance aircraft. And *this* is the way they want me to win the war."[248]

Lang, overcome with empathy for the field marshal, stayed quiet.

---

though, the aide recalls that "a little while after they had started, he swung around…" and made the remark. The quote in Ryan's book is also different than what was in the notes, which is presented here. [*Auth*].

As they rode along, Rommel was deep in thought about how he would organize the counterattack. He was stymied, though. So much, after all, would depend upon exactly where and how the enemy had landed and how far they had advanced. Had they been stopped? And if so, where? He could not even think about how to plan a defense until he had a complete picture of what was going on. And that would not happen until he arrived back at his headquarters, probably late in the evening.

A little after 4:30 p.m., Rommel reminded Daniel that they were going to stop in Rheims and phone in for some sort of update on what was going on. The driver replied that they would get there in less than a half-hour. Rommel nodded. Daniel was doing his best.

True to his word, at 4:55 p.m.,[249] the Horch rolled into the old city of Rheims, east-northeast of Paris. They pulled up to the city commandant's headquarters. Lang immediately got out of the car and went inside to call their headquarters at La Roche-Guyon. Rommel was close behind.

Entering the building, Lang quickly told the duty officer inside why they had stopped. Then he went to a nearby office and picked up a phone. He told the switchboard operator, "I want a state call[a] for Field Marshal Rommel to his headquarters."[250]

The operator complied, and a top priority state call went through to La Roche-Guyon.

After a minute or two to get connected, the chief of staff came on the line, and Lang said, "General Speidel? Field Marshal Rommel wishes to speak to you."[251]

---

[a] Like most overburdened communications systems, certain calls in the Reich were considered more important than others. A state call received very high priority, although it was not quite as critical as a *führungsblitz*

Rommel took the receiver and began talking. For the next fifteen minutes, they conversed as Speidel updated[252] him on the situation.[a]

Speidel's status report did not encourage Rommel at all. As a matter of fact, the more he listened, the more hopeless the situation seemed to get.

The enemy had established a series of beachheads along a 32-kilometer strip of coastline, from the northeastern base of the Cotentin peninsula to the Orne River. They had landed elements of some seven divisions, accompanied by a huge armada of warships. In addition, three or four airborne divisions had been dropped the evening before, two American in the Cotentin peninsula, and one or two British[253] near Caen.[b] Enemy air superiority, as Rommel had earlier predicted, was overwhelming.

Speidel continued with the bad news. Rommel groaned when he heard that the OKW panzer reserves (12th SS Panzer and *Panzer Lehr*) had only been released some 90 minute ago. As a result, elements of the 12th SS would not be able to reach the invasion area until the 7th, and *Panzer Lehr* would not be there until the 8th.

Summarizing, Speidel admitted that Normandy was indeed a large Allied operation. He added, "But it still doesn't rule out the possibility of a further major enemy invasion somewhere else!"[254] The chief of staff seemed to still feel that this was not the main invasion effort.

Rommel did not pursue that at the moment. He had already concluded in his mind that there would be no diversionary attack, but he did not want to waste time arguing with Speidel about that. Impatiently, he dropped the subject. He wanted to know about the panzers.

---

[a] Lang's account recalls the conversation as being 12 to 15 minutes long.

[b] Actually, it was only one division. The British 1st Airborne was not used.

"How far has our own counterattack progressed?" he asked. He was shocked to hear that there had been none as yet.[255]

"The 21st Panzer is ready," Speidel told him, "but it is awaiting further reinforcements before it advances."[a]

Rommel shook his head. What had happened to his counterattack-at-once instructions?!? "Get the division moving into the attack right now!" he barked.[256] "Don't await further reinforcements—attack at once!"[b]

After Speidel acknowledged, Rommel specifically ordered the 20th Panzer Regiment to engage immediately. He added that the 716th Division was to immediately regroup its forces. It was then to counterattack as well, all along the beaches.[257]

Lang left Rommel in private to finish up, and went outside to make sure that everything was ready for their departure.

Rommel emerged from the commandant's building a few minutes later. The conversation with Speidel had not taken more than fifteen minutes.[258] Lang could tell immediately by the look on the field marshal's face that he was quite upset. They piled back into the car, and Daniel started them off again, no one saying a word.[259]

The three of them traveled on in silence. Daniel was busy driving, and Lang did not dare intrude on the field

---

[a] Speidel was not updated yet on the attack developing against the British at Sword beach.

[b] Fraser's biography (*Knight's Cross*) leaves an entirely different perception of the conversation. Fraser indicated first of all that the call was made from Nancy, which is a considerable distance east of Rheims. Then he stated that Rommel phoned, "...to check that 21st Panzer Division... had been committed to counterattack. It had; at 7:30 a.m., five minutes after the most easterly (and nearest) enemy landings from the sea had touched down..." (Fraser, p. 487) While technically he is correct about the division's movements, the impression given of this passage is totally different than other sources.

marshal's thoughts. It was some time before Rommel began silently pounding one fist into the other. He did this on and off for a few minutes.

He finally turned around to his aide and said "If I was commander of the Allied forces right now, I could finish off the war in fourteen days!" He knew that he could, too.[260]

Having said that, and deep in thought, he turned back around and once again stared at the road ahead. Lang felt terribly upset and helpless. He was unable to provide the field marshal with any comfort.

Thinking about the possibilities, Rommel exclaimed, "God, I hope that there isn't a second landing right now from the Mediterranean."[261]

The landscape sailed by. Softly, he added, "I was right all the time…"[262]

Lang remained silent.

---

*By late afternoon, the crisis on Omaha beach was for the most part over. The sun had come out, and the light winds blowing in from the channel had thinned the haze and carried the smoky fog created by the gunfire and explosions inland. Allied bombers and fighters, now able to see their targets below, had renewed their attacks on the fixed German positions atop the bluffs and on key artillery positions inland, coordinating their attacks with the infantry.*[263]

*Ammunition for the surviving German coastal batteries had now nearly run out. With no supplies are forthcoming, they were forced to slacken or cease their fire. Allied sappers had finally blasted of holes in the anti-tank dike just below the bluffs. The Germans were now retreating from the beaches.*[264]

*The Americans at Utah Beach, not having had nearly as much trouble as their buddies on Omaha, were exiting the coast area in substantial numbers as they moved inland to join the fighting. Most of the German batteries on Utah had either been overrun or were out of ammo and had to be destroyed.*

*To the east of Omaha, British and Canadian troops had been moving inland since noon, and a couple of small towns had already been captured. The British were moving on to Bénouville,[265] while the Canadians were pushing pass Ver-sur-Mer, some 2-1/2 miles inland. The British airborne troops defending the Caen Canal Bridge had been relieved by Lord Lovat's commandos, linking the assault troops from the beach with the British 6th Airborne drop.*

*Meanwhile, the German panzer-grenadiers on the east bank of the Orne had fallen back...*

---

Rommel's car had just left Nancy, and Daniel was driving at a brisk pace as they continued back northwestward towards headquarters. All in the vehicle were all quiet except the field marshal, who made occasional repetitive comments.

"I knew I was right all the time," he said again, later in the afternoon. "I should have had both those divisions under my command to hit them right on the beaches."[266]

Occasionally, they had to go around a convoy, or stop at a checkpoint. Once in a while, low-flying enemy aircraft would slow them down. At times, his edginess getting to him, Rommel would impatiently smack one gloved fist into another.

At one point, his old rival on his mind, he said, "If Montgomery only knew the mess we are in, he'd have no worries tonight."[267]

A little later, he smirked and remarked bitterly, "My friendly enemy, Montgomery."[268]

Sometime later, Rommel tried to recover his hope. Perhaps it was not too late to change the outcome. If they could muster up their forces quickly enough, they might be able to stall the enemy long enough to bring in other units.

Speidel had reported that the 21st Panzer was getting ready to attack, although they should have already been committed. Anyway, if the panzers could punch through the advancing enemy infantry—Speidel had not mentioned anything about enemy artillery—they might make it down to the coast. The naval guns might not be that coordinated to the ground advance. So if the outdated but capable panzers of the 21st and a couple of assault battalions could get through the enemy line—and a night assault could, in the confusion, very possibly do that—they still might stop the British long enough to let the big panzer units nearby arrive and finish the job.[269] And if they could not drive the enemy back into the sea, they could certainly appreciably disrupt the enemy supply buildup.

If a section of the landing area could be rolled up, the other beachheads would have little chance of success. Especially if more units kept arriving every day. And until the Allies broke out and captured a port or more landing area, they'd be penned in and slaughtered, despite their overwhelming air and naval superiority. It just might work.

"My God!" he said aloud. "If Feuchtinger can only make it, we might be able to throw them back in three days."[270] Rommel was of course, trying to stay positive.

He was also having difficulty doing that.[271]

As he had said all along, time was the most critical factor. They had to drive the enemy back before he could establish his bridgehead and begin building his defenses. Time…

In the meantime, he was stuck riding along this damned road. Occasionally glancing at Daniel, Rommel impatiently urged his driver on, saying "Tempo! Tempo! Tempo!" The Horch surged ahead as Daniel gave the car more gas.[272] They were rushing through the French countryside, at times hitting speeds as high as 130 kph.[273]

Rommel stared on ahead at the road rushing towards them. He had to think.

# VI. D-Day: Evening
"Attack at once!"

*As the day progressed, squadrons of Allied tactical aircraft continued to swarm over the invasion area. Caen was bombed again (with a good number of the bombs missing the German positions altogether and smashing the center of the city), and Vire, some 30 miles to the southwest, would be hit at 8 p.m.[274] Also attacked by air were Cherbourg, Carentan, and Amiens.*

*German vehicles moving up to the front along inland roads were now getting repeatedly strafed by American and British tactical aircraft, while medium and heavy bombers continued to pound the defensive positions as darkness approached...*

*The Allies had now landed the staggering figure of over 150,000 troops onto French soil, controlling an area about 15 miles long, and almost six miles deep—over 80 square miles.[275] On the negative side, the casualties at Omaha beach seem terrible. They lacked about 50 percent of their men and vehicles, and about three-fourths of their heavy weapons and supplies, including tanks. The disorganized beachhead would not be able to withstand a determined panzer counterattack. The British were doing better, and before dawn would come, they will have landed the better part of four divisions.[276]*

*The expansive Allied fleet covered them from the Channel. The vessels were relatively safe from any German naval attack, although some three dozen U-boats would put to sea from the Bay of Biscay in the next 24 hours. None would reach the Allied shipping lanes for at least a week.[277]*

*Pitifully few German aircraft—maybe fifty or so of various types—had been available to scramble against the*

## VI. D-Day: Evening      Rommel's Fateful Trip Home

enemy landing, and those that had tried had mostly been thwarted by the overwhelming Allied air cover. Several aircraft attempting to pierce the umbrella had been shot down.[278]

In the meantime, the 21st Panzer Division was now fully committed in a gritty counterattack northward. The mobile units were determined to reach the Channel and then pivot to roll up the Allied flanks.

---

Rommel's command car rolled swiftly through the French countryside. Between the roadblocks, checkpoints, convoys, and the cows and goats blocking his path, the field marshal no doubt thought that he just might go insane. At one point, the car approached a couple cows angling across their pathway.

"Go around," Rommel said to Daniel. The driver swerved to the edge of the road and passed the cows and their owner, all of which had been surprised by the rapidly approaching black Horch.

Now again deep in thought, Rommel once again stared at the road ahead. Lang knew that he was terribly upset, but the aide could say nothing to comfort him. He continued his silence as the car sped on.

Evening was approaching.[279]

---

At Rommel's army group headquarters, Speidel was calmly reviewing the reports of the day, waiting for the field marshal to return and take over so that he could get some more sleep. One late message had him intrigued because it was designed to further muddle Army Group B's incomplete picture. The report stated that the channel just off the port of Dover was enshrouded in a smoke screen, and that another major operation could very well be expected there shortly.[280] The Allies were still playing the old shell game, and the Germans were going to be forced to have to deal with it, from the top on down.

---

It was some ten minutes after 9 p.m.[a] when Rommel's black Horch finally reached the village of La Roche-

---

[a] Like so many details of Rommel's trip home, the controversy over his return arrival at La Roche-Guyon continues among historians to this day. Captain Lang in his interview with Cornelius Ryan on July 9th, 1958, claimed that they arrived back at La Roche-Guyon at precisely 9:15 p.m. (CRC-26/25-Lang-9& notes) Ryan though, might have had some doubts about Lang's facts and omitted this exact arrival time in *The Longest Day* (pp.299-300). Samuel Mitcham (p.87), probably using David Irving as a source (p. 445), used the arrival time at the château of 10 p.m. Irving though, was probably going by British Double Summer Time, which has been used by most accounts. That would make the arrival time about 9 p.m., again converting to GCT. This time concurs with Lang's figure.

Strangely, Admiral Ruge in his *Reminiscences*, usually exact in stating his times (in typical Teutonic fashion—not always right, I found out occasionally, but nearly always exact) gives no specific arrival time, only mentioning that it was "in the evening" (p. 172). But in the admiral's interview with Ryan in Europe (May, 1958), he also specifies an arrival time of 9 p.m. (CRC-27/10, p.4) Interestingly, Ryan noted that Ruge had no diary available for him to see, although relentless biographer David Irving later made good use of Ruge's unpublished diaries (*Trail of the Fox*, p. 386), noting a number of "indiscretions" that Ruge seems to later have modified or 'remembered differently.'

George Forty (*The Armies of Rommel*, p.227) stated the arrival time was "2000 hours" (8 p.m.). Charles Marshall in his rather disorganized biography of Rommel, (p. 133) wrote that the field marshal's party arrived back at La Roche-Guyon at the unlikely time of 4:30 p.m. General Speidel himself (*Invasion 1944*, p.78) also gave the equally improbable time of "between 4:00 and 5:00 p.m." Given the distance, the fact that Rommel was definitely still home at 10:15 in the morning, the claim by Tempelhoff in his 1958 interview that the trip home (at normal *(Cont.)*

## VI. D-Day: Evening            Rommel's Fateful Trip Home

Guyon.[281] Daniel slowed down as they rolled quietly through the village. The town understandably was deserted.

The car finally turned off the main road, rumbled softly up the long driveway, and entered the courtyard of the well-guarded château headquarters[282] tires screeching as it stopped next to the main entrance.[283] Lang jumped out as the car came to a complete halt and ran ahead of the others up the main steps to inform General Speidel that they had returned.[284]

Hustling into the main hall, the aide slowed down, puzzled. Incredibly, he was hearing—yes, that was music! Baffled, he listened intently and soon recognized a Wagnerian opera. It was definitely coming from the chief of staff's office. Walking over, he saw the General Speidel standing in his doorway, listening pleasantly to the music.[285]

Stunned for a moment, anger began boiling up inside of Lang. The future of Germany was being desperately fought for out there, perhaps had even been lost by now, on the very beaches that this headquarters was assigned to protect. The field marshal was feeling miserable, tired, and laden with

---

speeds) had taken some 10 to 12 hours, (CRC-27.14) the later rendezvous with Lang, the heavy enemy air activity, and various other delays along the way, an arrival time before 8:30 p.m., even at breakneck speeds, seems unreasonable. The War Diary of *Heeresgruppe B* sadly lists no entry for their arrival. In fact, the first official indication in that document that shows Rommel has returned is an entry noted at 10:25 p.m., logging a phone conversation between the field marshal and General Dollmann, who commanded the Seventh Army at his headquarters south of the invasion area in Le Mans (CRC-26/5-14).

Lang's account seems the most realistic, reasonable since he actually made the trip. He also gives exact times to back his claim. Using his reporter's shorthand, Ryan wrote down Lang's testimony that: "On the outward journey from France to Germany it had taken them exactly twelve hours. On the return journey they left Freudenstadt at eleven and they finally arrived at La Roche Guyon that night at nine fifteen, so that the return journey took them only ten hours and fifteen minutes." (See first reference above.)

guilt for having been at home when it had all begun. And yet, the chief of staff was playing records.

Speidel saw Lang approach and came strolling out of his office, a look of serenity on his face.

Lang looked him straight in the eyes. He forgot for a moment that he was a captain speaking to a general as he asked in an incredulous tone, "General Speidel! The invasion! It's begun, and you're able to listen to Wagner?"[286]

Speidel, ever cool, smiled graciously in return and replied, "My dear Lang. Do you honestly believe that whether or not I am listening to Wagner would make any difference whatsoever to the course of the invasion?" Lang was too shocked to reply.[287]

Looking beyond the aide, the chief of staff saw the field marshal striding down the hall in his long blue-gray field coat, grim faced,[288] his baton gripped tightly in his right hand.[289] Briefly saying hello to Speidel, he walked directly past him into the chief's office and, with his hands clasped behind him, Rommel began studying the map. Speidel walked in and turned around to close the door, indicating that a conference was beginning. It was more than likely going to be a long one.[290] Naturally, Lang was not invited.

The aide stood there a moment, fatigued and dejected. It had been a terribly long drive, and the day seemed to be going horribly. Still, there was nothing that he could do right now—at least nothing that would help the field marshal.

Lang found his way into the dining room and collapsed at one of the tables. Tiredly, he stood up, poured himself a cup of coffee, and then sat down again. Gazing around the room, he spied another officer sitting in a chair, reading a newspaper. The other officer looked up affably, and asked, "How was the trip?"

Lang did not say anything. He could only stare at the man.[291]

## VI. D-Day: Evening          Rommel's Fateful Trip Home

As Speidel closed the conference room door, Rommel studied the situation map. Staring at the units and the busy arrows on it, he growled, "That's one hell of a mess."[292]

Speidel began his briefing, and as the field marshal listened, his concern over the situation kept deepening. On the right flank, the British had secured a beachhead 32 kilometers wide and some 4 to 10 kilometers deep. They threatened Bayeux in the center, which was barely holding on, defended by remnants of the shattered 915th Grenadiers.[293]

On the left flank, the Americans had broken through on the peninsula just northwest of the Vire Estuary[a] and were driving inland towards Ste-Mère-Église, which had been captured by American paratroopers. Along the lengthy strip of beach in front of Colleville, after a determined resistance, the onslaught of enemy assault troops coming ashore had ended. The Americans had somehow broken through the tenacious defenses on the cliffs and were now slowly but steadily moving off the beaches.[294]

Reports indicated that the Allies had landed at least six divisions, with elements of others starting to arrive. Three airborne divisions had been so far identified, two American landing on the Cotentin Peninsula, and one British landing on both sides of the Orne River. These *Fallshirmjäger* had secured the exits to the beaches in many places along both flanks of the invasion area.

German countermeasures were being put into effect. The enemy beach areas had been more or less sealed off, but front line units had taken a beating, and all of the reserves in the immediate area had been committed. Ammo was at a low level, and the men were struggling to hold on all along the

---

[a] Utah Beach [*Auth.*]

front without much support. Very few supplies were coming in, mostly because of the downed bridges along the Seine, and the overwhelming enemy air activity. Morale was down (Rommel personally blamed himself for that), and everyone was wondering where the hell the panzers were.[295]

The 21st Panzer had initially advanced northward upon the British paratroopers east of the Orne, and then, on Marck's orders, most of the division had regrouped, reversed direction southward, and had struggled for hours to move through the bomb-ravaged city of Caen to approach the British on the west.

They had then attempted to thrust north between the Canadian and British beachheads. The panzers though, had soon been stopped in their tracks by a number of anti-tank units positioned on a ridge. However, on their left flank, some panzergrenadiers had actually broken through the enemy lines and had reached the coast at one or two points, joining with the remnants of German units on the coast. They were currently exploiting the situation.[a]

On another positive note (Rommel was thankful for this one), *Panzer Lehr* and *12th SS Panzer Division* were finally on the road, moving up for a counterattack, although reports indicated that they were traveling slowly, and suffering casualties from many low-level air attacks. 2nd Panzer Division was to be moved down from the Somme area, and 2nd SS Panzer down in southern France was getting ready to trek northwards.

In the center of France, the 17th SS Panzergrenadier Division near the Loire River was also getting ready to move out and travel northward towards the invasion area. Thus, Rommel would gain at least three panzer divisions and one more panzergrenadier over the next few days to move against the enemy.[b] But would it be enough? Or was it

---

[a] Lt.Col. Joseph Rauch's 192nd Panzergrenadier Regiment.

[b] The 116th Panzer Division would for now remain near Paris, in case the
*(Cont.)*

already too late? According to what Rommel had been preaching all of these months, unless the Allies could be pushed back into the sea in the next few hours (highly unlikely), Germany had already lost the war. He hoped that he was wrong in this case. But he usually wasn't.

During the briefing, Rommel got on the phone with General Dollmann, the Seventh Army commander. The general, repeating what he had reported around 7 p.m., stated that the 12th SS was preparing to commit itself to action at 0700, while the *Panzer Lehr* was moving towards Thury-Harcourt,[296] about 30 km southwest of Caen.

He continued to give a full update of his situation as Rommel listened to him, occasionally taking notes.

While Rommel was on the phone with Dollmann's, Speidel called the chief of staff at *PanzerGruppe West*, *Generalmajor* Sigismund von Dawans. They talked about the commitment of the panzer group staff. Speidel told him that a decision on a date for the counterattack would be made on the 7th.[297]

His phone call over, Rommel stood silently looking at the map. Glancing at Speidel, who was now also off the phone and standing next to him silently, Rommel must have felt a twinge of guilt. The man had been forced to take on the field marshal's job on today, the most critical of all days. If they could not defeat the Allies, heads would probably roll, beginning with their own.

"Speidel," he said, looking back at the map, If I had been here, I could not have done anything else than what you have done, and the actions you have initiated."[298]

"*Danke, Herr Feldmarschall*," Speidel replied.

Rommel, depressed by the situation, told Speidel he was going to get something to eat. They both turned, left the room, and walked down to the dining room. Rommel noted that a few of the priceless Gobelin tapestries that covered the

---

enemy made a surprise strike to free the capital.

various walls of the château had been taken down off the walls.[a]

In the dining room, the field marshal was warmly greeted by several of his staff members, including Admiral Ruge (von Tempelhoff, who was traveling back separately, had not yet arrived). Hungry and depressed, Rommel sat down next to Lang at the dining room table. There, the two of them made a small supper out of a plate of cold meats. Tactfully, no one brought up the subject of the invasion. Despondent, it was far too heavy a topic for them all to delve into at that point. So they instead made idle chatter about his trip.[299]

About twenty minutes later, the meal finished, Rommel tiredly left the messhall and found himself in the hallway with his aide again. Lang was despondent. He was convinced that, had Rommel not gone home, the field marshal would have made all the difference. The invaders, instead of consolidating their landing areas, would be thrashing about in the surf, desperately trying to evacuate against a fearsome German counterattack.

Instead, their invasion now seems to have succeeded, or at best, threatened to succeed. According to Rommel's own theory, the first day would be the most crucial. Well, that first day was over. Had they already lost? Lang wondered.

It was now about 10:45 p.m. Rommel, going back to the situation room, was told that the Duty Officer at *OB West* had called fifteen minutes ago, with reports of several new glider landings. A hundred had been spotted near Falaise at 9:10 p.m. and many more had been seen at numerous points all along the Normandy coast, including Barfleur at the tip of the Carentan Peninsula, Isigny, and Caen. Many more though had been spotted coming down in the Le Havre area.

---

[a] According to Admiral Ruge, a few of the town's local inhabitants, "with whom Rommel's staff were on excellent terms," had started taking them down that day and packing them. (CRC-27/10, p.4).

Elements of the 21st Panzer, including the 200th Anti-Tank Battalion, were urgently asking for immediate reinforcements, especially infantry to support their panzer assault to the sea. Otherwise, they would not be able to hold their positions.

Rommel immediately called General Blumentritt at the villa he shared with von Rundstedt in St. Germain-en-Laye. Rommel, depressed, now pleaded to get the *Luftwaffe* committed. Blumentritt replied that OB West had already decided along with *Luftflötte 3* that the main air effort was to begin tomorrow, and would concentrate on the air space northwest of Caen.[300]

They then discussed chain of command for the panzers. Rommel asked him if the headquarters staff of *PanzerGruppe West* in Paris could take over some of the command burden of the beleaguered LXXXIV Corps. Blumentritt told him that they could and would. Rommel, satisfied, added that, in that case, his staff was thinking about assigning the low ground between Dives and Bayeux. Blumentritt though, echoing Speidel's earlier warning, cautioned Rommel that assaults on other coastal areas were likely and had to be kept under consideration.[301]

After getting off the phone with Blumentritt, Rommel called von Salmuth at Tourcoing about 10:50 p.m. The Fifteenth Army commander requested that the 1st SS Panzer Division, reorganizing in Belgium, be reassigned to him, so that they could protect the critical port of Antwerp. Rommel promised to support him and present the request to OB West.[302]

Rommel eventually called Blumentritt back just after midnight and forwarded his endorsement of von Salmuth's request. Blumentritt replied that they had already forwarded the request to OKW. Rommel made a note to tell Speidel to call Fifteenth Army and give them the news.[303]

Von Tempelhoff by now had arrived in his car with his own driver[a] and immediately had reported to General Speidel, who met him with a smile.[b] Von Tempelhoff told him that the trip back was uneventful, except for a few American bombers that flew by somewhere along the way. He told him that as he went across the Place de la Concord and onto the Champs Élysée, he noted how quiet and deserted the streets were.

After some time finding a place to gas up, they went on to headquarters. Speidel then briefed him on the situation, and when Rommel came in, they discussed it further.[304]

The field marshal said very little during this time. Finally, after a few moments of silence, Rommel remarked with a sigh, "Well, now it has happened. We'll just have to see it through."

A few minutes before 1 a.m., a call came in from *Major* Erich Vorwerk, the *Ic* at Seventh Army headquarters. He reported the sad news that the 21st Panzer's counterattack had failed and the division was withdrawing to positions south of Caen to dig in.

Although the panzers had been stopped by anti-tank units, the 192nd Panzergrenadier Regiment on their left flank had actually broken through to the coast at Lion-sur-Mer, had joined up with elements of the 736th Grenadier Regiment, and were now awaiting reinforcements to exploit their beach positions against the Canadians on their left and the British on their right.

Unfortunately, the enemy foiled their plans. An unexpected Allied air drop of about 500 gliders, with some of them carrying light tanks, had landed in their rear, in and

---

[a] Ryan in his interview at one point asked von Tempelhoff if he arrived back at headquarters at the unlikely time of 9 p.m., but von Tempelhoff, his mind on a previous question about meals with Rommel, never answered the question.

[b] "Always with a smile," Tempelhoff once said. (CRC-27/14-Tempehoff, p.38)

## VI. D-Day: Evening             Rommel's Fateful Trip Home

around the 21st's assembly area.[a] The division commander, Edgar Feuchtinger, fearing his men on the beach would be cut off and surrounded, had ordered them to pull back.[305] Rommel questioned that decision, but since it was already a *fait accompli*, there was no use in pursuing it.

They took another short break and four of them went out into the château's small park for a short walk; Rommel, Speidel, Ruge, and Lang. Lang walked behind the group at some distance back, and could not hear much of what was said. He could tell though that the field marshal was depressed over the failure of the 21st Panzer's counterattack. He noted the upset tone of Rommel's voice. At one point, Lang saw him sadly just shrug his shoulders, spread his arms, and open his fingers—a kind of resigned "what's the use" gesture.[306]

Over the next few hours, working well-past midnight into the next day, the field marshal tirelessly struggled to get updated on what had happened so far.

One of the first items on his agenda was to contact OKW and request that all the first-rate combat regiments from the Fifteenth Army be sent to Normandy, to be followed by the second-rate units at the Pas de Calais. OKW, now figuring that the main thrust was still yet to come, turned him down. They did though, allow him the use of the 346th Infantry northeast of Le Havre.[307]

Calling OKW back later, he requested that the 35,000-man garrison stuck on the Channel Islands be ferried to the mainland and moved to the front. OKW turned down his

---

[a] The force was actually about half that size, some 256 gliders. This was the 6th Airlanding Brigade. The third major unit of the British 6th Airborne Division, it was dropped around 9 p.m. only because there had not been enough aircraft to drop it and the division's two parachute brigades the night before. The unit carried an assortment of paratroopers, jeeps, light artillery pieces, light APCs, and a few light tanks. This stroke of luck on the British part essentially thwarted the only German panzer counterattack of the day.

request. If the Channel Islands were evacuated, the Allies could march right in and use them as a staging point for further smaller amphibious landings, not to mention create airstrips there.[308] Besides, he was reminded, the Channel Islands were a high political and psychological priority, because they were basically the only portions of original British territory that the Reich still controlled.

He also asked for operational control of the remaining two panzer divisions in the south[a] and the 17th SS Panzergrenadier Division on the Loire. Again, patiently, OKW refused his request,[309] even though the 17th SS was already getting ready to move north.

He then tried to contact a number of Seventh Army units, but most radio communications were being jammed, and many of the land lines were still out because of bombings and Resistance activities. He did though, at one point, get through to Max Pemsel at Seventh Army headquarters at St. Lô. "You've GOT to stop the enemy from getting a foothold, whatever happens!" he yelled into the phone.[310]

Despite communication problems, their phone center managed to get through to the 21st Panzer Division's headquarters. Rommel ordered them to attack the next morning at 8 a.m., along with the 12 SS Panzer which should be arriving by then.[311] Bayerlein's *Panzer Lehr* unfortunately had taken several casualties moving towards the invasion area, and it would take some time to get to get into the staging area, assemble, and prepare to attack.

The field marshal once more looked at the situation map. The 21st Panzer was dug in just in front of Caen and on the eastern flank. The 716th Division, reduced to the size of a regiment and just 12 pieces of artillery, was grimly hanging on. The 352nd just to the left of center was holding its own, but its supplies were running critically low, and no relief was

---

[a] The 9th and 10th Panzer Divisions.

## VI. D-Day: Evening                    Rommel's Fateful Trip Home

getting through to them. The division's engineer battalion, the last of the reserves, had moved from St. Martin-de-Blagny and joined the 916th Regiment, waiting for another attack in the Colleville area.[312]

The 1,000-man 30th *Schnell-Brigade* had left Coutances and was on its way to the front. Unfortunately, given the fact that they were traveling mostly by bicycle and were vulnerable to the heavy enemy air presence, they would probably not reach the invasion area until mid-morning.[313]

Other units had been alerted and were getting ready to move out. The mobile *Kampfgruppen* of the 275th and the 265th were preparing to move to Normandy. General Dollmann was going to move the mobile units from the 266th and all of the 77th Infantry Division as well, but Rommel wanted him to hold off on that for a bit. The enemy might just be waiting for that to happen, so that they could hit Brittany with a separate set of airborne landings. He did tell Seventh Army to keep the units on the alert for a possible move.[314]

---

It was well in the early morning hours before the field marshal took another break. Looking around, he saw that everyone around him was exhausted. They had all had a harrowing day, and it was obvious that they were ready to quit and go to bed.

The château by now was quiet, the workers having long departed for their quarters. At the front, as the night wore on, most activities out there had begun to wind down—except of course, the Allied buildup along the beaches; but even that was reported as slacking off some. A lot had happened, and tomorrow was going to be a very busy day indeed.

It was now nearly dawn at *Heeresgruppe B*, and the headquarters staff had made dozens of phone calls to various commands. Taking a break, Rommel walked out into the château's hallway and met Lang who was sitting out there, reading some reports.[a] The aide, too upset to sleep, wanted to be ready to help with anything. They had all by now heard of the repulse of the 21st Panzer's attack. Lang was crushed.

Looking at the field marshal morosely, he asked, "Sir, do you think we'll be able to manage it? Do you think we'll be able to hold them back?"[315]

Rommel, weary, glanced at him glumly and shrugged. Spreading his hands, he said, "Lang, I hope we can. I've always succeeded up to now."[316] But there was no conviction in his voice.

A while later, Rommel came across Lang again, still awake and studying reports. The field marshal looked at him and said gently, Well, Lang, you must be tired. Why don't you go to bed and get a good sleep."[317]

Lang agreed and retired as the field marshal went back into his office..

It had been a long day—the longest day, he had once called it. Well, that was certainly true for Lang and him.[318]

The exhausted field marshal turned away and, already lost in thought, slowly walked down the oak-paneled hall to his office.[319]

---

[a] There is also an unconfirmed story that local French inhabitants like to tell in which Rommel at some time after midnight strolled outside into the small park and there met the *Duc du Rochfoucauld*, whose family had owned the historic château for centuries, and who had been allowed to remain in the villa and live with his wife and daughter in upstairs quarters. Supposedly, the duke had said to him, "Well, Herr Field Marshal, I hear the invasion has begun."

Rommel supposedly had replied, "Yes, your Grace, and I think that your country will be free very very shortly." Although the two sometimes took walks together (surprising, since Rommel did not speak much French), von Tempelhoff told Ryan that he doubted this story was true. At any rate, the duke, who was over 60 years old, would hardly have been up in the early morning hours. (CRC-27/14-Tempelhoff, p.33)

His wife had turned fifty, and Germany had probably just lost the war—and both had happened at the same time.

# Epilogue

Rommel would struggle in vain for the next six weeks to push the Allies into the sea. He would try his best to regain the precious initiative that he had lost in those first fateful 24 hours. The enemy strength and resolve though, would prove to be too much.

Only twice more in his life would he ever meet with his one-time mentor, Adolf Hitler. The first meeting, some ten days hence, would be at an ad hoc war conference at the Führer's new but never used remote headquarters in Margival, France. Also attending would be Field Marshal von Rundstedt and their two chiefs of staff. The conference would center around the worsening military situation in Western France. At this conference, Rommel would take the opportunity to broach the idea of suing for peace, and Hitler, incensed that he would make such a plea, would angrily silence him.[a]

After that disappointing conference and disillusioned over his country's future, Rommel exhausted himself each day as he traveled up and down the Western Front, trying to stem the tide of enemy forces pouring ashore. The last time he ever saw Hitler was at a conference at the Berghof on June 29th. When Rommel suggested that the Reich should address the idea of some sort of political solution, he was brusquely told to leave the room. He never saw Hitler again.

He did though, start to consider the idea of throwing in his lot with the conspirators that he well knew were planning a coup (although he would never go for an assassination). Occasionally, he would even grumble about taking matters into his own hands.

However, on the afternoon of July 17th, while inspecting his positions near the front, as his command car

---

[a] See my book on this meeting, "Crossroads at Margival."

traveled along an open road in the French countryside, the Desert Fox's famed luck would finally run out. The complex course of his life collided with the deadly, impersonal trajectories of a strafing British Spitfire's cannon shells. Rommel was mortally wounded and suffered a massive head injury when his Horch skidded into a tree and he was thrown from the car onto the highway. Mortally wounded, bleeding intensely, and painfully drifting in and out of consciousness, he was taken to a hospital and would be unaware of the famous attempted assassination of the Führer that would take place just three days later at Hitler's headquarters in Rastenburg.[a]

Struggling to recuperating from his wounds, Rommel for nearly three months would sit out the war, first in the hospital, and eventually back at his home in Herrlingen—until his indirect involvement with the anti-government plotters would become exposed, and he would be forced by Adolf Hitler, once his mentor and champion, to meet his destiny on October 14th, 1944 through a forced suicide.

---

[a] Sources record that Rommel's first reaction when he heard about the assassination attempt was one of horror. Most of his concern was that Hitler's murder would turn the dictator into a martyr for the SS and his close thugs to rally around. Part of the shock though, was the very brutality of the act. And part of course, was his reaction as a loyal German officer to the idea of a coup against the leader of Germany—his commanding officer, and one-time mentor and friend.

# German Terms Used

*Abwehr*— The *Wehrmacht's* Intelligence security service that specialized in counterintelligence.

*Armeegruppe*—A small, sometimes ad hoc army group; It was usually an army command of one large army and some odd units or two small adjacent armies. It often fell under the auspices of the area Heeresgruppe. Because it was smaller or possibly temporary, an Armeegruppe did not rate the full administrative support a Heeresgruppe was given.

*Blitzsperren*—Lit. 'Lightning fields.' Special minefields that were to be laid by all available vessels immediately as soon as the invasion was impending. (S.160, qq.37)

*bodenständige*—Static. A somewhat informal term used to denote German "static" (limited field mobility) infantry divisions serving in France (e.g., the 709th Grenadier), under Field Marshal von Rundstedt's reorganization of 1942. This type division was almost exclusively used for coastal defense, garrison or occupational duties. A static division was similar in makeup to the German standard triangular infantry division, in that it consisted of nine infantry battalions, but they were usually smaller in size and made up of second-rate or third-rate troops such as POWs, overage conscripts, 'liberated' foreigners (who often could not even speak German), or recovered casualties. A *bodenständige* division did not have a recon battalion, and only three (and not the customary four to six) artillery battalions (non-motorized), and very little (if any) transport.

*Fallschirmjäger*—A paratrooper. Parachute units were equipped with the latest weapons and played a critical part against the Allies after the Normandy invasion in 1944, functioning as ad hoc battle groups. By then, their role was limited to being élite assault units, due to the crippled nature of the *Luftwaffe*. However, they still kept the honorary designation of being airborne.

*Fingerspitzengefuehl*—An almost-eerie, sixth sense that gave one the ability to sense upcoming danger, a hidden problem, or even an enigmatic change to take advantage of a situation. Supposedly, Rommel had it on the battlefield.

*Feldgrau*—Lit. 'field gray'. Nickname for the average German soldier; derived from the field-gray color of their uniforms.

*Flak*—Short for *Flugzeugabwehrkanone*. A German anti-aircraft gun or unit. Flak units were created at the beginning of the war to create concentrated zones of anti-aircraft fire, either at key positions, or in urban areas. A *Flak Regiment* (FlakR) at this time in the war usually mobile (*Sturm*), and was comprised of three or more Flak battalions.

*Fremde Heere West*—Foreign Armies West. The intelligence branch of the Army High Command, responsible for finding out the Allied ground order of battle, and the main intelligence source for lower commands.

*Führer*—Lit. 'Leader.' As an adjoining word, it referred to a unit leader or commander. Used alone, it was a term in the Third Reich reserved exclusively for the German commander-in-chief, Adolf Hitler. This title gave reference to this individual as the supreme head of the Nazi Party the German state, and of course, the armed forces. Hitler took the title after Hindenburg's death. In doing so, he was indicating that the positions of Chancellor and President were being combined. The complete title that he used was *Der Führer und Oberste Befehlshaber der Wehrmacht des Grossdeutschen Reichs.*

*Führerbefehl*—A direct order from Adolf Hitler. It carried the highest priority and importance, to be executed immediately.

*General der <xxx>* —The rank of general; equivalent to U.S. Army rank of lieutenant general. This German rank required the individual's specialty be included, unlike most other ranks. Types included: *Infanterie* (Infantry), *Artillerie* (Artillery), *Kavallerie* (Cavalry), *Panzertruppen* (Armored), *Pioniere* (Engineers), *Flakartillerie* (Anti-Aircraft), *Luftwaffe* (Air Force), and *Fallshirmtruppen* (Paratrooper).

*Generalfeldmarschall*—Field marshal. This historic title (shortened form is *Feldmarschall*) was the highest normal rank possible in the *Wehrmacht*; equivalent to U.S Army rank of General of the Army. In 1942, a special collar patch for this rank was introduced. A German field marshal supposedly had the rare privilege of being able to request a private, personal audience with Hitler whenever he desired.

*Generalleutnant*—German Army rank of lieutenant general; equivalent to U.S. major general.

*Generalmajor*—German Army rank of major general; equivalent to U.S. Army rank of brigadier general.

*Generaloberst*—German Army rank of colonel general; equivalent to U.S. Army rank of 4-star general.

*Heeresgruppe B*—Army Group B. A German *Heeresgruppe* was an army command consisting of two or more armies. Army Group B consisted of the German 7th Army covering northwest France, the 15th Army covering northeastern France, and the German occupational forces in the Low Countries.

*Hitlerjugend*—The 'Hitler Youth.' This was the paramilitary youth association created and strictly controlled by the Nazi Party in 1933 as a way to indoctrinate and motivate males from 14 to 18 years old into Nazi culture and ideals, and to prepare them for military service, especially into the SS (*Schutzstaffel*). Hitler Youth corps were also used though, to provoke, torment, roust and otherwise discriminate against various groups targeted by Nazi doctrine, such as religious organizations and ethnic groups (especially the Jewish population).

*Heereswaffenamt (HWaA)*—The Armaments Office of the German Army. Created in 1919 and located in Berlin, its mission was to develop and oversee production of German weaponry. Used before World War II to rearm the *Wehrmacht*, its focus later was to create better weapons and weapon production to fight the enemy.

*Ia*—First General Staff Officer in a German unit headquarters, equivalent to the U.S. Army G-3. The Chief of Operations, he oversees command and control of the command's units.

*Ic*—Third General Staff Officer in a German unit headquarters, equivalent to the U.S. Army G-2. He oversees all matters relating to intelligence, including gathering, analyzing, and presenting it.

*Kampfgruppe*—Battlegroup. A loosely-assigned unit created from improvised combat units of various sizes. They were usually named after their commanders.

*Konteradmiral*—A rank in the German Navy, equivalent to a U.S. Navy rear admiral.

*Kriegsmarine*—The German Navy.

*Luftflötte*—Air Fleet. Corresponding to a numbered American Air Force unit, it was a major, self-sustaining. military unit in the German Air Force, consisting of up to a thousand aircraft, and having its own supply maintenance, transport, and administrative units. The *Luftwaffe* consisted of several *Luftflötten*, each comprised of two to four *Fliegerkorps*, each of these performing a specific function.

*Luftwaffe*—The German Air Force.

*Nebelwerfer*—Literally "fog or smoke launcher. Originally, the term referred to a 100-mm mortar that fired a chemical weapon, such as gas or smoke. Unlike the First World War though, gas or chemical attacks were outlawed and never to be used. Thus, in the years before the war, the units were modified to operate small mobile rocket launchers for use against concentrations of light infantry. For intelligence purposes, the term remained for the rocket units that replaced these weapons as a ruse to fool the Allies.

*OB West—Oberbefehlshaber West.* Supreme Command, Western Theatre. Using this title, Field Marshal von Rundstedt had operational control of all *Wehrmacht* forces in Western Europe.

*Oberfeldwebel*—German army rank of master sergeant.

*Oberst*—German army rank of colonel.

*Oberstleutnant*—German army rank of lieutenant colonel. Equivalent of lieutenant colonel in the U.S. Army.

*OKW—Oberkommando der Wehrmacht,* the German Combined Armed Forces Supreme Headquarters. Its location moved to wherever Hitler was currently staying, be it Berchtesgaden, his advance headquarters *Wolfsshanze I* in Eastern Prussia, or Berlin. Since he was currently at the Berghof in Lower Bavaria, OKW was located in and around the nearby town of Berchtesgaden.

*Östentruppen*—Lit. 'Eastern troops.' A term that referred to Russian or East European prisoners of war or in some cases, 'liberated' soldiers who had been coerced into switching sides to fight for Germany. Technically they were not an actual type of unit; rather, their units were usually classified as either infantry or cavalry types and deployed as such. Thus, an *Öst Bataillon* was an infantry battalion that was usually composed of an odd mixture of Russians, Hungarians, Latvian, and Polish prisoners of war or deserters.

*Panzer Lehr*—Lit. "Armored Training/Demonstration." A specific German panzer division, one of the few designated just by name, and considered one of the best in the German Army. It was formed to act as a critical bulwark against the upcoming Allied invasion of France, but its creation in the view of many historians was considered a critical mistake, because manning it pulled experienced training instructors and troops out of the schools and put them into combat.

*panzergrenadier*—A term used to refer to armored infantry, which nearly always was a component of either a panzer division, or a panzergrenadier division. The men moved and fought with armored transport vehicles such as halftracks, prime movers, and armored cars.

*PanzerGruppe West*—Armored Forces Command, Western Theatre. Commanded by General Geyr von Schweppenburg.

*PzKw—PanzerKampfwagen* (Lit. "armored battle vehicle"). The German formal term for a tank. Corresponding to the U.S. term 'Mark,' it denoted a model number when followed by a Roman numeral. Thus, the Allies term of Mark IV was based upon the German counterpart, *PanzerKampfwagen IV, (PzKw IV).*

*Wehrmacht*—A term used to describe the combined German military armed forces from 1935 on. Although the term was often erroneously used to refer to just the German Army, it included all the armed forces, consisting of the German Army (*Heer*), Navy (*Kriegsmarine*), and the Air Force (*Luftwaffe*). For ground operations, The *Waffen-SS* were tactically a part of the *Wehrmacht* as well. The term has over the years been modified to *Wehrmacht* in English texts (omitting the 'h') and is not only now generally accepted but more commonly used. However, it is an illiterate spelling alternative that began as a non-standard, improper variant of the original term.

*Wüstenfuchs*—"Desert Fox." The term coined in 1941 for Erwin Rommel because of his early successes in North Africa against the British.

# Reference Notes

A good part of the information that was used in this article came from just a half dozen distinct sources. First and foremost was the amassed material of interviews, logs, official documents, and well-detailed data collected by Cornelius Ryan for his classic, *The Longest Day*. A surprisingly vast amount of information, I discovered to my astonishment (and delight) had never made it into his classic account. Among this material were three detailed personal interviews of this trip home, given by Helmuth Lang, Hans-Georg von Tempelhoff, and Rommel's two immediate family members: his wife Lucie-Marie, and his son Manfred.

My heartfelt thanks to Douglas McCabe, curator of the Cornelius Ryan Collection at the Alden Library of Ohio University, Athens, Ohio for his cooperation, his insight into the material and into Ryan's methods, and for his unswerving assistance in helping me gather the information that I needed.

My second major source was *Trail of the Fox*, written by the now-controversial David Irving. Despite the furor that was raised over his later claims about the Nazis, Irving was and remains one of the most fastidious, detailed researchers ever, a trait I confirmed in several talks with him. This biography of Rommel is perhaps one of his greatest works, a book that stands as an impressive piece for this or any period. Unfortunately, I did not get a chance to access Irving's microfilmed notes. They I am sure would have provided me with even greater detail of this part of the field marshal's life. My thanks to Mr. Irving for his encouragement in pursuing more details of the field marshal's life.

Other major sources used included Ruge's detailed reminiscences, Fraser's biography, Rommel's own papers, and Harrison's excellent account of the invasion.

# Bibliography

The Cornelius Ryan Collection (CRC), Ohio University, Alden Library, Athens, Ohio—Douglas McCabe, Curator. Specially-accessed source material from this collection is coded as such. Mr. Ryan stored all of his materials for his three classic books (*The Longest Day*, *A Bridge Too Far*, and *The Last Battle*) in numbered boxes, each in turn being divided into folders. Thus, for example, reference CRC-26/25-Lang-3 is from the Cornelius Ryan Collection, the Lang interview, page 3, located in the twenty-fifth folder of Storage Box #26.

Canadian National Defence Headquarters **(CND)**, Ottawa, Canada, Report No. 50—The Campaign in North-West Europe, Information from German *Sources—Part II: Invasion and Battle of Normandy (6 Jun to 22 Aug 44)*, Directorate of History, Historical Section (G.S.), Army Headquarters.

Astor, Gerald, *June 6, 1944, The Voices of D-Day*, St. Martin's Press, New York, NY, 1994.

Berger, Sid, *Breaching Fortress Europe - The Story of U.S. Engineers in Normandy on D-Day*, Society of American Military Engineers, 1994.

Breuer, William B., *Hitler's Fortress Cherbourg*, Stein and Day, NY, NY, 1984.

Brown, Anthony Cave, *Bodyguard of Lies*, Harper & Row, NY, NY, 1975.

Buffetaut, Yves, *D-DAY SHIPS - The Allied Invasion Fleet, June 1944*, Naval Institute Press, Annapolis, MD, c. by Brassy Ltd, 1994.

Carell, Paul, *INVASION - They're Coming!* E.P. Dutton & Co., NY, NY, 1963, Revised Edition, Schiffer Publishing Ltd., Atglen, PA, 1994, trans. by David Johnston. Originally published as *Sie Kommen!* by Verlag Ullstein Gmbh, Berlin.

Chicken, Stephen, *OVERLOARD COASTLINE: The Major D-Day Locations*, Biddles Ltd., Woodbridge Park, Guildford, Sussex, England, 1993.

Drez, Ronald J. ed, *Voices of D-Day*, Louisiana State University Press, Baton Rouge, LA, 1994.

Forty, George, *The Armies of Rommel*, Arms and Armor Press, London, 1997.

Fraser, David, *Knight's Cross: A Life of Field Marshal Erwin Rommel*, Harper Collins Publishers, NY, NY, 1993.

Harrison, Gordon A., *Cross-Channel Attack*, U.S. Army in World War II, The European Theater of Operations, Office of the Chief of Military History, U.S. Department of the Army, Washington D.C., U.S. Government Printing Office, 1951.

Hastings, Max, *OVERLORD: D-Day and the Battle for Normandy*, Simon and Schuster, NY, NY, 1984.

Hooton, E.R., *Eagle in Flames: The Fall of the Luftwaffe*, Brockhamp-ton Press, London, England, 1997.

Irving, David; *The Trail of the Fox* (Softbound), Avon Books, NY, NY, 1977.

Isby, David C., ed., *Fighting the Invasion: The German Army at D-Day*, Greenhill Books, London, England, 2000.

Keegan, John; *Six Armies in Normandy*, Viking Press, NY, NY, 1982.

Kershaw, Robert J., *D-Day - Piercing the Atlantic Wall*, U.S. Naval Institute Press, Annapolis, MD, 1994.

Lewin, Ronald; *ROMMEL: As Military Commander*, Van Nostrand, Reinhold Company, NY, NY, 1968.

Lewis, Jon E. (editor), *Eyewitness D-Day: The Story of the Battle by Those Who Were There*, Carroll & Graf Publishers, Inc., NY, NY, 1994.

Liddell-Hart, BH, *The German Generals Talk*, William Morrow, NY, NY, 1948, 1975.

Luck, Hans von, *Panzer Commander: The Memoirs of Colonel Hans von Luck*, Dell, NY, NY, 1989.

Majdalany, Fred, *The Fall of Fortress Europe*, Doubleday and Co., NY, NY, 1968.

Man, John, *The D-Day Atlas - The Definitive Account of the Allied Invasion of Normandy*, Facts on File, Inc., 1994.

Mark, Eduard, *Aerial Interdiction - Air Power and the Land Battle in Three American Wars*, U.S.A.F. Special Studies, Center for Air Force Studies, 1992.

Marshall, Charles F., *Discovering the Rommel Murder: The Life and Death of the Desert Fox*, Stackpole Books, Mechanicsburg, PA, 1994.

Mitcham Jr., Samuel W., *The Desert Fox in Normandy: Rommel's Defense of Fortress Europe*, Praeger, Westport, CN, 1997.

Mitchie, Allen A., *The Invasion of Europe - The Story Behind D-Day*, Dodd Meade & Co., NY, NY, 1964.

Nafziger, George F. (1), *The German Order of Battle: Panzers and Artillery in World War II*, Stackpole Books, Mechanicsburg, PA, 1995 & 1999.

Nafziger, George F. (2), *The German Order of Battle: Waffen SS and Other Units in World War II*, Stackpole Books, Mechanicsburg, PA, 1995 & 1999.

Patrick, Stephen A., *The Normandy Campaign, June and July, 1944*, Gallery Books, NY, NY, 1986.

Ryan, Cornelius, *The Longest Day*, Simon and Schuster, NY, NY, 1959.

Reuth, Ralf Georg (Marmore, Debra S. and Danner, Herbert A, translators), *Rommel: The End of a Legend (Rommel, Das Ende einer Legende)*, Haus Books, London, England, 2005 (Original: PoperVerlag GmbH, München).

Reynolds, Michael, *Steel Inferno - 1 SAS Panzer Corps In Normandy*, Sarpedon, NY, 1997.

Richards, Denis, *The Hardest Victory - RAF Bomber Command in the Second World War*, W.W. Norton & Company, NY, NY, 1994.

Rommel, Erwin, *The Rommel Papers*, B.H. Liddell Hart, ed., Hartcourt Brace & Co., NY, NY, 1953Ryan, Cornelius; *The Longest Day*, Simon and Schuster, NY, NY, 1959.

Ruge, Friedrich, *Rommel in Normandy: Reminiscences*, Presidio

Press, San Rafael, CA, 1979.

Stillwell, Paul (editor), *Assault on Normandy*, U.S. Naval Institute Press, Annapolis, MD, 1994.

Von Falkenhausen, General Alexander von, *Von Falkenhausen 1922-1945*, 012554-MS B-289, U.S. Army, Foreign Military Studies Office, Carlisle Barracks PA., December, 1946.

Westphal, Sigfried, *The German Army In The West*, Cassell, London, 1951.

Wilmot, Chester, *The Struggle for Europe*, Collins, London, England, 1952.

Wilson, Theodore A., *D-Day 1944*, The Eisenhower Foundation, The University Press of Kansas, Lawrence, KS, 1971 & 1978.

Young, Desmond, *Rommel: The Desert Fox*, Berkley Books, London, England, 1950.

## About the Author

By profession, Peter Margaritis has been a technical writer for nearly 30 years. A native of Columbus, Ohio, he minored in History at The Ohio State University, where he graduated in 1978 with a bachelor degree in Business. He has an extensive military background, served in the U.S. Navy in communications, and before retiring as a chief petty officer, worked for twelve years in Naval Intelligence.

Peter is a writer who has studied the concepts of war for 50 years, specializing in the European military campaigns of World War II. He has given several private lectures on World War II and the Civil War. Although he has written many technical manuals and guides as a civilian, countless reports in and about the military, and several articles on World War II and the Civil War, he has only now started the process of publishing.

# Other Titles By This Author

**Articles**
- Crossroads at Margival: Hitler's Last Conference in France, June 17, 1944
- The Night the Sky Blew Up: Clan Fraser and the Destruction of Piræus Port, April 6, 1941
- Bust Eisenhower: The Story of the Message That Almost Ruined D-Day
- Reichsfibel: Ein Lexikon von Militär & Politische Akronyme und Ausdrücke von Das Drittes Reich
- A Brief History of MTA
- Grognard
- The Toledo War

**Books**
- 90 Years of History: The American Legion In Central Ohio
- Countdown to D-Day—The German Perspective; Part One: Der Atlantikwall
- Countdown to D-Day—The German Perspective; Part Two: Les Sanglots Longs

# Endnotes

## I. JUNE 1ST THROUGH 3RD

[1] Mitcham, p.49.
[2] Liddell-Hart, p.238.
[3] Mitcham, p.55.
[4] Brown, p.619.
[5] Majdalany, pp.346-7, and Brown, p.617.
[6] *Ibid.*
[7] Reynolds, p.301, Mitcham, p.57.
[8] Harrison, p.242.
[9] Isby, p.48.
[10] Harrison, p.131, Liddell-Hart, p.238.
[11] Ruge, p.65.
[12] Liddell-Hart, p.238.
[13] Ruge, p.168.
[14] Richards, p.233.
[15] Harrison, p.261.
[16] Irving, pp.422-423.
[17] Drez, p.51.
[18] Ruge, p.168.
[19] Fraser, p.510.
[20] Ruge, p.168.
[21] U.S. Army, MS B-289.
[22] *Ibid.*
[23] *Ibid.*
[24] Keegan, p.134.
[25] Ruge, p.168.
[26] Irving, p.422, CRC-27/8, p.1
[27] Ruge, p.168.
[28] *Ibid.*
[29] Richards, p.233.
[30] Brown, p.638.
[31] *Ibid.*
[32] Ruge, p.169.
[33] Mitcham, p.58.
[34] CRC-26/4:MS-X.548, p.3.
[35] Ruge, p.169.
[36] Luck, p.170.
[37] Ruge, p.168.
[38] CRC-26/26, pp.1-2, and from that, Ryan, p.33.
[39] Harrison, p.275.
[40] Ruge, pp.168-9.
[41] Irving, p.423.
[42] CRC-27/21, pp.1-3. Von Rundstedt was probably at his villa on this day.
[43] 'Marshal Bubi'. Ryan, p.22.
[44] *Ibid*, pp.16-17.
[45] CRC-26/4:MS-X.566, p.3 & MS-X.548, p.2 (from the *OB West* War Diary).
[46] CRC-26/4:MS-X.548, p.2.
[47] Irving, p.423.
[48] *Ibid,* Carell, p.16.
[49] Irving, p.423.
[50] Carell, p.36, Irving p.354.
[51] Ryan, pp.16-17.
[52] Mitcham, p.60.
[53] *Ibid*
[54] This famous quote, repeated in the movie "The Longest Day," was supposedly made some time in February. (CRC-26/4, p.1)
[55] *Ibid*
[56] Carell, p.89 and Drez. p.53.
[57] CRC-26/4:MS-X.548, p.2.
[58] Irving, p.423, and Mitcham, p.60.
[59] Lewin, p.223 and Carell, p.20.
[60] Mitcham, p.60.
[61] Harrison, p.272f and Carell, p.71.

[62] Patrick, p. 41 and Harrison, p.272.
[63] Patrick, p.41.
[64] Breuer, p.59.
[65] Carell, p.71, and Ryan, p.39.
[66] Carell, p.12, Mitchie, p.140.
[67] *Ibid.*
[68] Patrick, p.41, Breuer, p.62.
[69] Ryan, p.13.
[70] Brown, p.637, Breuer, p.74.
[71] Ryan, pp.13-14.
[72] *Ibid.*
[73] Irving, p.398.
[74] Brown, p.637.
[75] Ryan, p.15.
[76] Irving, p.389.
[77] Ryan, p.21, Brown, p.637.
[78] Brown, p.637.
[79] Ryan, pp.15-16.
[80] Irving, p.405.
[81] Ryan, pp.15-16, Irving, p.405.
[82] Ryan, p.19.
[83] CRC-26/25-Lang, p.1.
[84] *Ibid.*
[85] CRC-26/25-Lang, p.1 and Irving, p.399.
[86] Ryan, pp.18-19.
[87] Ryan, p.16.
[88] Fraser, p.479 and CRC-26/25-Lang, p.1
[89] Ryan, p.19.
[90] CRC-27/14-Tempelhoff, p.9.
[91] Ryan, p.19-20, and CRC-26/25, p.5.
[92] *Ibid,* CRC-26/25, p.1.
[93] These conversations are taken from Ryan's notes.
[94] *Ibid.*
[95] Brown, p.638.
[96] Ryan, p 18.
[97] Ryan, p.21. Mitcham, p.63, Brown, p.638.
[98] Ryan, p.21, Breuer, p.75.
[99] Carell, p.11, Ryan, p.21.
[100] Brown, p.637.
[101] Ryan, p.19.
[102] Ryan, p.30.
[103] CRC-26/25, p.1.
[104] Mark, p.251.
[105] Mark, p.251.
[106] Ryan, p.21.
[107] CRC-26/25, p.2.
[108] *Ibid.*
[109] Ryan, p.35 and CRC-26/25, p.3.
[110] CRC-26/25, p.3.
[111] Ryan, p.35.
[112] CRC-27/14-Tempelhoff, p.1.
[113] Ryan, p.35 and CRC-26/26, p.4.
[114] *Ibid.*
[115] CRC-26/25, p.4.
[116] Ruge, p.169.
[117] *Ibid.*
[118] CRC-26/25, p.4.
[119] Ryan, p.36.
[120] Ryan, p.35 and Ruge, p.169.
[121] *Ibid* and Brown, p.638.
[122] CRC-26/25, p.5.
[123] *Ibid.*

[124] *Ibid.*
[125] *Ibid.*
[126] CRC-27/13, p.4.
[127] CRC-26/25, p.5.
[128] *Ibid*, Carell, p.23.
[129] Mitcham, p 1, 30, 53, 97.
[130] CRC-27/18, p.1.
[131] Ruge, p.169.
[132] Brown, p.638.
[133] CRC-26/25, p.6. Most of the details of the trip here are taken from Ryan's interview of Lang and of Tempelhoff. Ryan's *typewritten* notes show the quote as, "How can I tell Hitler that, although he gives many orders, they are not implemented." However, the quote in the text comes directly from Ryan's *handwritten* notes.
[134] CRC-26/25, p.6.
[135] *Ibid.*
[136] CRC-26/14-Tempelhoff, p.9.
[137] CRC-26/25, p.6.
[138] *Ibid.*
[139] *Ibid.*
[140] *Ibid.*
[141] CRC-27/14-Tempelhoff, p.8.
[142] CRC-26/25, p.7.
[143] CRC-26/25, p.6.
[144] CRC-26/25, p.7.
[145] *Ibid.*
[146] *Ibid.*
[147] Irving, pp.399.
[148] CRC-26/25, p.7, CRC-27/14, p.11. Col. von Tempelhoff's version varies slightly from Lang's. In his interview with Ryan in March of 1958, nearly fourteen years after these events, von Tempelhoff had a bit of trouble remembering some of the trip details. Lang's memory was much better, although he had left the motorcade some time before this point, taking the second car to his home. At any rate, von Tempelhoff remembers his parting with Rommel: "Near Ulm… Maybe I dropped into his house. I don't remember this… nevertheless, I left him there, and drove further down to Munich." If this is true, then Tempelhoff would have had to secure another vehicle somewhere, unless Daniel drove him.
[149] Marshall, p.2
[150] CRC-27/8-LMR, p.2, CRC-26/25, p.8. Ryan in his notes identified the dachshund as Ajax, perhaps based on the interview. Both puppies had been given to Rommel as a present by the Todt Organization back in January, 1944. However, the older Ajax had turned out to be the much more aggressive of the two. Rommel had finally taken him home when he went on leave in February, so that Lucie-Marie could take the time to train him. Ajax unfortunately though, was run over by a car

in May, so Elbo had been sent home to cheer up Lucie-Marie. Treff had been given to Rommel as a replacement dog on May 5th.
[151] CRC-27/8-LMR, p.3.
[152] *Ibid.*
[153] *Ibid.*
[154] *Ibid.*

## III. JUNE 5TH

[155] Ryan, pp.60-1 and Harrison, pp.272-3.
[156] *Ibid*, Majdalany, p.356.
[157] Source: Berger, p.79.
[158] Harrison, p.274.
[159] Ryan, p.62, Harrison, p.274.
[160] Ryan, p.90.
[161] Wilson, p.109.
[162] Rommel, p.471, Mitcham, p.71, Carell, p.56, Buffetaut, p.17.
[163] Carell, p.56, Ryan, p.90.
[164] Patrick, p.42.
[165] Ruge, p.171.
[166] Irving, p.205.
[167] Ruge, p.171 and Ryan, p.80.
[168] The figure is Ryan's. Brown, p.641, stated that it was 22 pages long.
[169] Ryan, p.80.
[170] Breuer, p.75, and Majdalany, p.357. Fifteen-year old Manfred, who had been drafted back in early January, (Mitcham, p.32) was currently serving in the *Luftwaffe* Auxiliary. He was assigned to an anti-aircraft unit in Stuttgart. He obtained leave to go home to be home with his father.
[171] CRC-27/8-LMR, p.3. and Brown, p.643.
[172] CRC-27-14-Tempelhoff, pp. 14-16.
[173] Ryan, p.20, Fraser, pp.485.
[174] CRC-27/8-LMR, p.4.
[175] Rommel, p.471.
[176] Mitcham, p.62.
[177] Ruge, p.172, CRC-27/23, p.3.
[178] CRC-27/23, p.3.
[179] Irving, p.436, Brown, p.641.
[180] *Ibid.*
[181] Irving, p.437.
[182] Rommel, p.471, Drez, p.88.
[183] Drez, p.99, Mitcham, p.142.
[184] Ryan, p.107.
[185] Ryan, p.105, Harrison, p.279.
[186] Brown, pp.647-8.
[187] Irving, p.438.

## IV. JUNE 6TH - MORNING

[188] Irving, p.438.
[189] Keegan, p.134, Patrick, p.54, and Breuer, p.88.
[190] Lewis, p.93, Astor, p186, and Breuer, p.89.
[191] Carell, p.90, Drez, p. 179.
[192] Carell, pp.112-13.
[193] Fraser, p.491.
[194] Drez, p.126.
[195] Harrison, p.304.

[196] Astor, p.222.
[197] Chicken, p.9.
[198] Carell, p.80.
[199] *Ibid*, Patrick, p.77.
[200] Buffetaut, p.114.
[201] Buffetaut, pp.114-18, Lewis, p.116, and Keegan, p.135.
[202] Irving, p. 440.
[203] Ryan, pp.151-152.
[204] Ryan, p.258.
[205] Mitcham, p.90, off Carell, pp.114-15.
[206] Irving, p.441, CRC-27-8, p.4.
[207] *Ibid.*
[208] Irving, p.423.
[209] CRC-26/25, p.4.
[210] Mitcham, p.76, from Ryan, pp.284, CRC-26/5-WD, p.7, Irving, p. 442, CRC-26/25, p.8, and CRC-27/8, p.4.
[211] CRC-27/8-MR, p.4.
[212] CRC-27/8-Koch, p. 5.
[213] CRC-27/8-MR, p. 4 and Koch, p.5.
[214] CRC-27/9-Koch, p.5.
[215] CRC-27/8-MR, pp.4-5.
[216] CRC-26/25, p.8
[217] CRC-27/14-Tempelhoff, p.18.
[218] *Ibid.*
[219] *Ibid.*
[220] *Ibid.*
[221] CRC-27/14-Tempelhoff, pp.24-26.
[222] CRC-27/8-LMR, p.5.
[223] CRC26-25, p.8.
[224] Irving, pp.441-42.
[225] *Ibid.*
[226] Ryan, pp.284-85.
[227] *Ibid*, CRC-26/25, p.8 and Irving, p.442.
[228] CRC-27/8-LMR, p.5.
[229] Ryan, p.285.
[230] Irving, p.442.
[231] *Ibid.*
[232] Ryan, p.285, Irving, p.444.
[233] Ryan, p.285.
[234] Irving, p.442.
[235] CRC-26/25, p.8
[236] CRC-27/8-LMR, p.5.
[237] CRC-26/8-LMR, pp.5-6.
[238] Irving, p.442.
[239] *Ibid.* CRC-27/8-FMR, p.7, and Irving, p.442.
[240] Irving, p.444.

## V ROMMEL HEADS BACK

[241] Irving, p.439.
[242] Irving, p.444.
[243] Ryan, p.294.
[244] Marshall, p.249.
[245] CRC-26/25, p.8 and Ryan, p.294.
[246] CRC-26/25, p.10 The time that this comment was made is not given, other than it was "on the way back."
[247] Ryan, p.294.
[248] CRC-26/25-Lang, p.10.
[249] Irving, p.444, Ryan, p.296, CRC-26/25, p.8, Mitcham, p.87, CRC-26/5, p.14.
[250] CRC-26/25, p.9. The original notes of Ryan for some reason show the two additional words "to you."
[251] *Ibid.*

252. Irving, p.444, Ryan, p.296, CRC-26/25-Lang, p.9.
253. Irving, p.444.
254. *Ibid.*
255. *Ibid.*
256. *Ibid.*
257. CRC-26/25-Lang, p.9.
258. CRC-26/25-Lang, Original notes.
259. Ryan, p.296.
260. Mitcham, p.84 fm Ryan, p.297 which is in turn fm CRC-26/25-Lang, p.9.
261. CRC-26/25-Lang, p.10 The time of this comment is not given, other than it was "on the way back."
262. CRC-26/25-Lang, p.9.
263. Breuer, pp.97-8.
264. Keegan, p.144.
265. Lewis, p.135.
266. CRC-26/25-Lang, p.9.
267. CRC-26/25-Lang, p.10 Like a couple other quotes, the time of this comment is not given, other than it was "on the way back." However, putting it just before the second "Montgomery" comment seemed logical.
268. *Ibid*, Ryan, p.296.
269. *Ibid.*
270. *Ibid*, CRC-26/25-Lang, p.9.
271. Ryan, p.296.
272. Ryan, p.294.
273. CRC-26/25-Lang, p.9.

## VI. D-DAY: EVENING

274. Lewis, p.158.
275. Irving, p.445 and Marshall, p.133.
276. Mitcham, p.87.
277. Wilson, p.165.
278. Harrison, p267.
279. Ryan, p.296.
280. Irving, p.445.
281. *Ibid*, CRC-26/25-Lang, p.10.
282. Ryan, pp.299-300.
283. Irving, p.445.
284. Ryan, p.300 and CRC-26/25-Lang, p.10.
285. CRC-26/25-Lang, p.10.
286. Ryan, p.300, CRC-26/25-Lang, p.10. The words used are those that were given in the actual interview, which varies slightly from the exact words that finally ended up in Ryan's book. In *The Longest Day*, Ryan quotes Lang as asking, "How can you possibly play opera at a time like this?"
287. Ryan, p.300 from his CRC-26/25-Lang, p.10. Again, the interview varies from the book text. Ryan must have been exercising a little poetic license, perfectly normal back then. In Ryan's book, Speidel's reply was changed to, "My dear Lang, you don't think that my playing a little

music is going to stop the invasion, now do you?"
[288] Irving, p.445.
[289] Ryan, p.300.
[290] *Ibid.*
[291] *Ibid.*
[292] CRC-27/8-Koch, p.6.
[293] Mitcham, p.91, fm Harrison, p.338.
[294] Mitcham, pp.90-91.
[295] Rommel, pp.474.
[296] CRC-26-5/MS.X-511, p.17.
[297] CRC-26-5/MS.X-511, p.18.
[298] CRC-27/8-Koch, p.6.
[299] CRC-26/25-Lang, p.11.
[300] CRC-26-5/MS.X-511-18, pp.18-19.
[301] *Ibid.*
[302] *Ibid.*
[303] *Ibid.*
[304] CRC-27/14-Tempelhoff, pp.19-22.
[305] CRC-26-5/MS.X-511, p.19.
[306] CRC-26-25-Lang, p.11.
[307] Mitcham, p.85.
[308] Majdalany, p.364.
[309] *Ibid.*
[310] Irving, p.445.
[311] Irving, p.445 and Mitcham, p.91.
[312] Harrison, p334.
[313] *Ibid.*
[314] *Ibid.*
[315] Ryan, p.301, CRC-26/25-Lang, p.10 Again, Ryan is playing with his notes. The modified book quote is, "Sir, do you think we can drive them back?"
[316] Ryan, p.301, CRC-26/25-Lang, p.10 Unlike the original interview, the book quote adds the word "nearly" before the word "always," exaggerating the presence of doubt that must have been in Rommel's mind.
[317] CRC-26/25-Lang, p.11. Again, Ryan modified the quote in the book. The changed version there is, "You look tired," he said. "Why don't you go to bed? It's been a long day." Ryan, p.301.
[318] Ryan, p.301.
[319] *Ibid.*

Printed in Great Britain
by Amazon